Cultures of Erudition and Desire in University Pedagogy

T0352805

This book promotes adult education in a university setting as cultivation and the inculcation of culture, democracy, and ethics beyond and through lived experience. It draws on theories from across disciplines, bringing together Aristotelian and post-structuralist thought. This includes Fernando Pessoa's notion of 'erudition' as culture and 'disquiet' as a mode of contemplative living, with Fernand Deligny's 'wanting' as manifestation of life. Liana Psarologaki addresses the pathologies of life and higher education in advanced capitalist societies and creates a manifesto for a new type of university pedagogy.

Liana Psarologaki is an architect, artist, educator, and creative scholar based in the UK.

Rethinking Education
Series Editor: Bernd Herzogenrath and Tim Ingold

In the face of the still dominant model of progressive education, the volumes in this series explore ways of thinking education otherwise – ways that give hope for coming generations and for the renewal of life. They offer visions for the future, manifestos, experimental curricula, speculative syllabi, and case studies of alternative education at work. They are short and provocative, intended for academics, researchers, professionals and students alike.

Young Children Visit Museums
Cultural and Creative Perspectives
Margaret Carr, Brenda Soutar, Jeanette Clarkin-Phillips, Leanne Clayton, Bronwen Cowie, and Shelley Butler

Cultures of Erudition and Desire in University Pedagogy
Thoughts on Practice-led Curricula Before, Through, and Beyond Deleuze
Liana Psarologaki

For more information about this series, please visit
https://www.routledge.com/Rethinking-Education/book-series/RETHED

Cultures of Erudition and Desire in University Pedagogy

Thoughts on Practice-led Curricula Before, Through, and Beyond Deleuze

Liana Psarologaki

LONDON AND NEW YORK

First published 2023
by Routledge
4 Park Square, Milton Park, Abingdon, Oxon OX14 4RN

and by Routledge
605 Third Avenue, New York, NY 10158

Routledge is an imprint of the Taylor & Francis Group, an informa business

© 2023 Liana Psarologaki

British Library Cataloguing-in-Publication Data
A catalogue record for this book is available from the British Library

Library of Congress Cataloging-in-Publication Data
Names: Psarologaki, Liana, 1983– author.
Title: Cultures of erudition and desire in university pedagogy : thoughts on practice-led curricula before, through, and beyond Deleuze / by Liana Psarologaki.
Description: Abingdon, Oxon ; New York, NY : Routledge, 2023.
Series: Rethinking education | Includes bibliographical references and index.
Identifiers: LCCN 2022015009 (print) | LCCN 2022015010 (ebook) | ISBN 9781032073125 (hardback) | ISBN 9781003220619 (ebook)
Subjects: LCSH: Education, Higher—Aims and objectives. | Adult education. | Adult college students | Experiential learning. | Open scholarship. | Capitalism and education.
Classification: LCC LB2322.2 .P75 2023 (print) | LCC LB2322.2 (ebook) | DDC 378.001—dc23/eng/20220521
LC record available at https://lccn.loc.gov/2022015009
LC ebook record available at https://lccn.loc.gov/2022015010

ISBN: 978-1-032-07312-5 (hbk)
ISBN: 978-1-032-11588-7 (pbk)
ISBN: 978-1-003-22061-9 (ebk)

DOI: 10.4324/9781003220619

Typeset in Times New Roman
by Apex CoVantage, LLC

To Each and All My Students and Teachers

Contents

Rethinking Education   ix

Introduction, or 'for a 15%'   1

  Notes 5

PART 1
Tuber: Entering the Root   7

  "I Have Not Finished School" 8
  Playing Dostoyevsky's Idiot: "But-why?" 10
  Ecosystemic Idiocracy 11
  An Illness of One's Own 13
  A Tale of Viruses and Nerves 14
  Notes 16

PART 2
Synapsis I: Aristotle, Pessoa, and the Missing
Cultures: Erudition   19

  Scholē and Tedium 21
  The Impotent Scholar 23
  Desire to Defer? 24
  To Currere 26
  Notes 28

PART 3
Synapsis II: Deligny and Deleuze; Post-Humanist Desires   31

Post-Humanist Citizenship 33
In-Between Democracy 35
Desire Networks 37
Utopian Currere 38
Notes 40

PART 4
Synapsis III: Maverick and Temperate;
A People-In-Becoming   43

The Vocation of Becoming Anthropos 45
Ignorance and Disengagement 46
Maverick and Temperate 48
A People-in-Becoming 50
Notes 52

PART 5
Rhizome: Erudition in Times of Apnoea; Educating
an Ill Generation   55

Index   61

Rethinking Education
Series Editor Foreword

Education is the way a society produces its own future. But what sort of future is this? For more than three centuries, in the Western world, it's been wedded to an ideal of progress. A progressive education, according to its advocates, makes it possible for advances in human knowledge, forged by bringing the powers of the intellect to bear upon the material of empirical observation, to be passed from one generation to the next. Thanks to education, they insist, each generation can stand upon the shoulders of its forbears, contributing thereby to the ascent of civilisation as a whole. Empowered by the voice of reason, the educated are authorised to speak on behalf of a world whose sheer factuality subtends the vagaries of human experience. Here, in the community of reason, everyone is interchangeable. Problems have their right answers, and it makes no difference who comes up with them.

But what if the dream of progress turns out to be a chimera? What if our much-vaunted civilisation is but a castle in the air, that leaves behind a world in ruins? Has progress, in its mission to wipe out difference and to measure the achievements of every generation by a universal standard, been achieved at the expense of human flourishing, and more than that, of the flourishing of all forms of life? Is it too much to dream of another sort of future, not of progress but of renewal – a future that would afford room for everyone and everything to thrive in this wondrous planet we all share, both presently and forever? For in this, surely, lies the proper meaning of sustainability. Whereas progressivists imagine every generation as a layer, each adding to the one before, in an education for sustainability, generations would not so much be stacked vertically as wound longitudinally, like the overlapping fibres of a rope. It would be in their very overlap that the work of education is carried on.

Could this be what education is really about: learning to live together in difference? The very word education, after all, comes from the Latin *ex-* ('out') plus *ducere* ('to lead'). Education literally leads us out into the world. And as a way of leading out, it is fundamentally a practice of exposure. Its purpose is not to arm ourselves with knowledge, or to shore up our defences so that we can better cope with adversity. It is rather to disarm, to relinquish the security of established standpoints and positions, and by the same token, to attend more closely to the world around us and respond to what we find there with skill and sensitivity. Its primary commitment, in short, is to the fostering not of rationality but response-ability. If the voice of reason belongs at once to everyone and no one, with response-ability every voice is different, yet as in a choir or conversation, it comes forth only through its participation with the voices of others.

This kind of education doesn't separate knowledge from life, but joins with the very forces of life – forces that create ideas, ways of experiencing the world – in its ongoing fashioning. In their education, teachers and students embark together on a journey that may be difficult, even uncomfortable, with no certain outcome. This calls for care, patience, and a willingness to experiment. Nevertheless, the journey is one in which generations can collaborate in finding a way into the future. It is not, then, for teachers to transmit knowledge readymade. Their task is rather to set an example, to serve as constant companions for their students and tireless critics of their work. And it is for students to follow in their footsteps while improvising a passage for themselves.

In the face of the still dominant model of progressive education, the volumes in this series explore ways of thinking education otherwise – ways that give hope for coming generations and for the renewal of life. They offer visions for the future, manifestos, experimental curricula, speculative syllabi, and case studies of alternative education at work. In line with Routledge's *Focus* series, they are short and provocative, intended for academics, researchers, professionals, and students alike. We hope these volumes will convince our readers that other ways are possible!

The Editors

Introduction, or 'for a 15%'

On 15 February 1963 a prohibited students' protest took place at the Propylaea of the National and Kapodistrian University in Athens. Students carrying documents presenting a petition of one million signatures' demand that the state ensures 15% of its annual budget is allocated to education (παιδεία). The protest became disorderly and violent as two thousand police force under orders by the Ministry of Education broke in the event which brought further political turmoil.[1] The national press featured the events prominently and widely while similar protests regarding wider political affairs took place at the same time in Europe and the USA. At that time the post-war mid-class generation started enjoying the luxury of securing life-long tenured civil servant jobs as a direct perk of having a University degree and could therefore become more preoccupied with leisure and consumption (Sorey and Gregory, 2010:190). On 17 November 1973, students and political activists of the left wing protested for the triplet of commons of 'bread-education-freedom' (ψωμί-παιδεία-ελευθερία) against the military dictatorship of 1967 (calling itself The Revolution). At the culmination of the protest, which started at the School of Law, they gathered at the main entrance of the National Technical University of Athens on Patision Ave. which is now the campus for its world-renowned School of Architecture. Later that day many of them would die under the caterpillar treads of the government's military tanks. This was the most documented scene of the Greek post-war *Junta*. I remember myself commemorating this event annually together with my classmates and teachers during my twelve years of compulsory education and in September 2001, I went through the threshold of that same gate to enrol on the School of Architecture. Soon after I realised that the school would occasionally be occupied by leftish activists and the mentality of its student body was dominated by a subculture of disquiet and anger often steered pretentiously by collectives external to the school who claimed to safeguard the academic asylum – the right of the university

DOI: 10.4324/9781003220619-1

campus for educational freedom. After a long battle with violence and vandalism in university campuses nationwide, and within a climate of economic and moral recession in 2009, five distinguished academics signed an open letter for its abolition.[2] The debate continues.

During my student years at the National Technical University of Athens and before coming to the UK for postgraduate study, I was immersed in an everyday reality of regular protests, the occasional tear gas, and Molotov rackets. I experienced a studentship of war, anger and disquiet which grew into me as a feeling of tiredness and indifference. Twenty years later, now being an educator, I am taken over by a similar disquiet that sometimes leads to boreout and sometimes to burnout. Apparently both terms are now scientifically defined as neural conditions, which I continue to recognise not only on myself but also on my peers. At the same time, student protests in the USA and southern Europe continue not only in the liberal bastion type of Universities, but across many types of campuses and institutions. Overall, the university student body (if something like this exists) is also reportedly becoming less socially engaged with the commons and more isolated when in campus (Sorey and Gregory, 2010:185) with much systemic-generated disquiet expressed through online communications and on social media. Often this will concern the prerogative of each individual student for no surprises under the protection of consumer rights,[3] and various triggers of apolitical dissatisfaction in the educational service provided by a university, sometimes legitimately disguised under anonymity and momentarily justified by the dictum 'one has nothing to lose'. In the last five years of teaching at University, I observed and reflected upon patterns in the expression of disquiet related to the student prerogative (of being an enrolled student) and its counterpart of in-class/in-campus lived experience of being a student, active studentship – a kind of scholarship. The observation pertained classes of different subjects taught on undergraduate and postgraduate level, student engagement in quality assurance processes, student feedback, course validation, and student mentorship and was synthesised with an eclectic literature review and pedagogical research conducted through pilot studies and experimental curricula (Psarologaki, 2014) and which brought a key interest in clinical and critical studies related to education and particularly the study of the notion of aboulia and disquiet (Rabinbach, 1992:156).

I started using the term disquiet within a pedagogical context after reading *The Book of Disquiet* by Portuguese poet Fernando Pessoa, following a student trip and conference presentation in Lisbon in 2019. The Book of Disquiet (Pessoa, 2010) is a fragmented memoir published posthumously and translated and curated diversely and by many, in which Pessoa's notes present disquiet as a deeply human condition of being as a result of chronic tedium and associates these with its everyday life in the city of Lisbon, therefore the civic life, the commons and the polis, linking what one would read as existential dread with democracy and education. For the latter, Pessoa uses the term translating into erudition, a cultivation through education – παιδεία. Reading on the political dimension of studentship in different situated contexts, for instance the student activism in Africa (Nyamnjon et al., 2012) and Asia (Weiss and Aspinall, 2012), I realised these were deeply concerned with political reform and societal values but did not receive the treatise of their like in the 60s and 70s that took place in western countries, and my concern grew over the idleness of the political ontology of education and its pedagogical ramifications, today. Experiencing and *doing* education, (being learner and educator) has been lately characterised by neurological crisis. Historian Anson Rabinbach, who writes on the pathologies of the individual in modern life and their links to education, is right to assert that such malady is beyond its 'modern aetiology, a modernism of the symptoms and the narrative of the illness itself' (Rabinbach, 1992:161) and that aboulia can be a non-habitation of a will that remains uneducated. With this book, I aim to take this further and assign not an aetiology but a symptomatology that concentrates on issues of a culture of tedium and disquiet in pedagogy and desire (in relation to will and the intellect). Based on the observations and experiences mentioned earlier, this book is an investigation on critical pedagogies and curriculum philosophy that hopefully do not remain detached from the educational reality and life in and out of scholarship.

The term critical pedagogy was coined by pedagogist and cultural critic Henry A. Giroux (2020) who through his philosophy advocates education for active citizenship where 'progressive educators might redefine their roles as engaged public intellectuals capable of teaching students the language of critique and possibility as a precondition for social change' (Giroux, 2020:89). Giroux also observed a shift from education of emancipation (modern) to a pedagogy of resistance (postmodern) through which a critical and a border pedagogy may emerge respectively. This distinction is similar to what Rosi Braidotti highlights in the work of Deleuze and Foucault between the politics and the political; 'politics is made of progressive emancipatory measures predicated on chronological continuity, whereas the political is driven by transformative collective actions that require the non-linear time of critical praxis' (Braidotti, 2018:289) which is later defines as *schole*. The latter, as with a border pedagogy, offers the opportunity to learners to 'engage knowledge as border crossers . . . [where] . . . the terrain of learning becomes inextricably linked to the shifting parameters of place, identity, history and power' (Giroux, 1991:72). This is a nomadic topos of a pedagogy (Roy, 2003) where the participants in and facilitators of the learning (the educational relata) not only cross the borders of identity (immigrants) but become accountable for understanding the identities and non-identities of others, forming networks of a people-in-becoming (nomads). 'Whereas the migrant leaves behind a milieu that has become amorphous and hostile, the nomad is one that does not depart . . . who clings to the smooth space left' (Deleuze and Guattari, 1987:381). The cartography of such pedagogy this book offers a glimpse of as related university vocational curricula is based on 'coordinates of becoming . . . implicated in the immanent plane whence entities, events, and individuations arise' (Roy, 2003:81), which create an ecology of a pedagogy that is critical and clinical (Radman and Sohn, 2018) and based on the study of symptoms that according to Deleuze can produce new entities if attuned to desiring production (Tynan, 2010:153).

The book follows a rhizomatic structure with neural references, in three synapses (Parts 2, 3 and 4) and two radices (Part 1 and 5) and follows the methodological stance of 'dirty theory', which is a feminist ecological perspective established by Helene Frichot (2019) in the critical use of an assemblage of sources and research findings of variant matter that may come from assumingly scarce areas. It builds its themes drawing from an eclectically interdisciplinary pool of meta-philosophies and post-theories and addresses the pathologies of life and higher education in advanced capitalist societies. Most prominently it reflects on the principles of education as achievement of *The Burn Out Society* by Byung-Chul Han (2015) and the pathologies of learning highlighted in *Capitalist Realism* (2009) by Mark Fisher. It transcends conventional (yet still significant) educational approaches such as the reflective practitioner by Schön and focuses uniquely on adult learning philosophy of pedagogies. It presents no singular or exhaustive contribution to the philosophy of education, educational theory, or pedagogy of practice. Like Semetsky and Masny in their book *Deleuze and Education* (2013), I also find these as 'three interconnected problematic fields' (Semetsky and Masny, 2013:1) but I am attempting a radical rhizome as synthesis instead of a line of flight and a fold. This book uses an eclectic synthesis of these three fields with a uniquely shaped pedagogical perspective coming from teaching and creating curricula in disciplines that is vocational and academic, inherently relevant to the Deleuze, and offers 'onto-ecology or counter-cartography' (Wallin, 2013:35) looking at Fernand Deligny's and his work *The Arachnean and Other Texts* which has been generally overlooked perhaps because he was not a specialist (in education or philosophy), yet he served as one of important references for Deleuze and the concepts of nomad and symptom, which I will reference through theories of desire in pedagogy (Zembylas, 2007 and Webb, 2019). Part 1 (Tuber: Entering the Root) starts with an ecological approach to pedagogy and a contextual definition of pedagogical praxis in reference to ethical and political dimensions of human life. Part 2 (Synapsis I: Aristotle, Pessoa, and the Missing Cultures: Erudition) explores the constitutive elements of education and erudition with a focus on a cultural ecology of learning. Part 3 (Synapsis II: Deligny and Deleuze; Post-Humanist Desires) situates desire in the cartography of the learning process and highlights the importance of citizenship and networks by reading Fernand Deligny from a posthuman perspective. Part 4 (Synapsis III: Maverick and Temperate; a People-in-Becoming) unfolds the characteristics of a learners' network as a-people-to-come and unfolds two profiles of nomad scholars as educational relata: the maverick and the temperate. The concluding Part 5 (Rhizome: Erudition in Times of Apnoea; Educating an Ill Generation).

This book has been an attempt to create fissures of thought by becoming a self-reflecting practitioner – a scholar of one's own scholarship – and as such to allow this pedagogical research to be led by (academic) practice. I have drawn from my experiences at the School of Architecture Engineering of the National Technical University of Athens, the University of Northampton, Technical University Delft, the Architectural Association, and the University of Suffolk, and at the Royal Institute of British Architects. The book was shaped by insightful discussions of the highest academic rigour and depth with colleagues at my affiliated institutions and beyond, including Prof Nic Bury, Dr Sara Biscaya, Doina Carter, Ming Cheng, Ben Powell, Dr Marco Spada, Dr Andrej Radman, Bryan Wybrow, and Dr Stamatis Zografos, as well as the inspiring thoughts and practices of Prof Sean Griffiths, James Soane, and Rosi Braidotti. This book is about and for a generation of educators and students who have been and continue to be emotionally and physically strained by the fetters of systemic stagnation often disguised as ad nauseam inexorable processual changes, and for that 15% which students in Athens protested for back in the 60s, and which was since forgotten and now settled as one of the lowest in the EU at 4% in 2022.[4]

Notes

1 www.kathimerini.gr/k/100yk/1031860/diadilosi-gia-to-15-stin-paideia/
2 www.universityworldnews.com/post.php?story=20190702070215123
3 www.gov.uk/government/publications/higher-education-guide-to-consumer-rights-for-students
4 www.ethnos.gr/greece/article/187570/dapanesgiapaideia18hsthneehelladame 425toyaepproblepshgia2022

References

Braidotti, R. (2018) 'Generative Futures: On Affirmative Ethics' in A. Radman and H. Sohn (eds.), *Critical and Clinical Cartographies: Architecture, Robotics, Medicine, and Philosophy. New Materialisms.* Edinburgh: Edinburgh University Press. 288–308.

Deleuze, G. and Guattari, F. (1987) *A Thousand Plateaus: Capitalism and Schizophrenia*. Trans by B. Massumi. London: Athlone Press.

Fisher, M. (2009) *Capitalism Realism; Is There No Alternative?* Winchester: Zero Books.

Frichot, H. (2019) *Dirty Theory: Troubling Architecture, (The Practice of Theory and the Theory of Practice)*. Baunach: ADDR – Spurbuchverlag.

Giroux, H. A. (1991) 'Border Pedagogy and the Politics of Modernism/Postmodernism' in *Journal of Architectural Education*, Vol. 44 (2), 69–79.

Giroux, H. A. (2020) *On Critical Pedagogy*. 2nd ed. London: Bloomsbury.

Han, B.-C. (2015) *The Burnout Society*. Stanford, CA: University of Stanford Press.

Nyamnjon, F. B., Nkwi, W. G. and Konings, P. (eds.) (2012) *University Crisis and Student Protests in Africa: The 2005–2006 University Students' Strike in Cameroon*. Mankon and Bamenda: Langaa Research and Publishing.

Pessoa, F. (2010) *The Book of Disquiet*. London: Serpent's Tail.

Psarologaki, L. (2014) 'Conjunctive Synthesis as an Interdisciplinary Pedagogical Method for Art and Design – a Cube' in *The International Journal of Arts and Sciences*, Vol. 7 (3), 613–624.

Rabinbach, A. (1992) *The Human Motor: Energy, Fatigue, and the Origins of Modernity*. Berkeley and Los Angeles: University of California Press.

Radman, A. and Sohn, H. (2018) 'The Four Domains of the Plane of Consistency' in *Critical and Clinical Cartographies: Architecture, Robotics, Medicine, and Philosophy. New Materialisms*. Edinburgh: Edinburgh University Press. 1–20.

Roy, K. (2003) *Teachers in Nomadic Spaces. Deleuze and Curriculum*. New York: Peter Lang.

Semetsky, I. and Masny, A. (2013) *Deleuze and Education (Deleuze Connections)*. Edinburgh: Edinburgh University Press.

Sorey, K. C. and Gregory, D. (2010) 'Protests in the Sixties' in *College Student Affairs Journal*, Vol. 28 (2), 184–206.

Tynan, A. (2010) 'Deleuze and the Symptom: On the Practice and Paradox of Health' in *Deleuze Studies, Special Issue on Deleuze and the Symptom*, Vol. 4, No. 2. Edinburgh: Edinburgh University Press. 153–160.

Wallin, J. (2013) 'Get Out from Behind the Lectern; Counter-Cartographies of the Transversal Institution' in D. Masny (ed.), *Cartographies of Becoming in Education; A Deleuze and Guattari Perspective*. Rotterdam: Sense Publishers.

Webb, D. (2019) 'Utopian Pedagogy: Possibilities and Limitations' in *Pedagogy, Culture & Society*, Vol. 27 (3), 481–484.

Weiss, M. L. and Aspinall, E. (eds.) (2012) *Student Activism in Asia: Between Protest and Powerlessness*. Minneapolis: University of Minnesota Press.

Zembylas, M. (2007) 'Risks and Pleasures: A Deleuzoguattarian Pedagogy of Desire in Education' in *British Education Research Journal*, Vol. 33, 331–347.

Part 1
Tuber
Entering the Root

'Every act of and in education, however small, comes from a context'
(Cole, 2021:104)

Pedagogy in its wider sense has only recently started being studied systematically as an ecological concept, as an element of an ecosystem or as being ecological. When Felix Guattari first published *The Three Ecologies* (1989) the world was only starting to look forward to a new millennium by means of technological anticipation (and the emergence of the first mobile phone) for the glory of a future that is yet to come and the World Wide Web was just launched at CERN, changing forever our access to and dissemination of information. By its first translation in English (2000), many in the Westernised world with access to everyday contemporary technology became habitually preoccupied with watching Big Brother live, feeling disappointed that Y2K, the famous 'millennium bug', did not actually bite them.[1] Twenty years later, Guattari's ecosophy is quoted widely in environmental and pedagogical philosophy as most of the population suffers from the educational inadequacy to fathom, respond to, and act against what is a global pandemic with not only immunological ramifications but most notably causing neurological crisis, economic lacunae and exposing deep environmental, pedagogical, and institutional maladies. Cultural curriculum theorist Jason J. Wallin notes reading on Guattari's work for and in La Borde that 'emerging illnesses [are] an effect of the institution itself' (2014:127). As such, we must return to the primal habitat – the oikos – for an eco-pedagogical change.

To speak about ecological and pedagogical change, it is important to define and (re)frain pedagogy, highlighting its relative positioning with (almost a topology of) learning and education, and ecology through sustainability. David R. Cole in his book *Education, the Anthropocene, and Deleuze/Guattari* defines education from a deleuzoguattarian perspective as 'an encounter, a nexus between teaching and learning, wherein something

DOI: 10.4324/9781003220619-2

happens, which we might call an event' (2021:104). This event, he argues, is heterogenous (a synthesis). It takes place in-situ but is not site-specific, and has become entwined in global capitalism, rendered through the lens of life-long-learning. In such a system, Alain de Botton notes, 'the phrase "I have finished School" would sound extremely strange' (2020:22) and insists on a culture that would opt for intuition and less for analysis (2020:257). This is effectively picked up also by Wallin who sees institutionalised and standardised education as a place that neglects by analysis and imposes an ontological risk to pedagogy. Highlighting the importance of social patterns outside school to education in the work of Guattari, Wallin asserts that peda-gogical transformation and change 'does not entail the dissolution of the school, but rather its assemblage with non-institutional social relays and initiatives capable of modulating why and how pedagogy might happen' (2014:137). This is also well rooted in Ted T. Aoki's 'curriculum-as-lived' as opposed to 'curriculum-as-planned' (2005:161), which we will refer to in this book as 'currere' and which will entail 'co-operative council, non-mandatory classes, [and] heterogenous student groupings' (Wallin, 2014: 132–133). We can talk therefore about an ecology of education as peda-gogy. Reading the Guattarian ecology, Verena Andermatt Conley offers an interpretation to Ernst Haeckel's definition of ecology as 'systems theory of the living' (2009:61) highlighting the etymological root of the term ecology as the logos (λόγος) of oikos (οίκος): the literary study of the lived; a peda-gogy od disclosure that spans from the domestic to the cosmic.

"I Have Not Finished School"[2]

This book approaches education and pedagogy from an ecological thought perspective and uses ecosystemic terms to address thoughts on the cultures of learning, teaching and the lived experience of being in education. Fur-thermore, this book offers tools and thinkables (Frichot, 2018:149) for a transformation in pedagogy. Such are oriented towards sustainable futures which are not bound necessarily by specific green agendas. On the contrary, the are radical because they emerge by revisiting and reflecting on the root of what is a complex abstract machine. Like David R. Cole's *Education, the Anthropocene, and Deleuze/Guattari* (2021) this book is not contextu-alising a genealogy of pedagogy to then propose transformations. Follow-ing Deleuze-Guattari it does not create plateaus of immanence either. It formulates synapses of thought by synthesis that are achronous and there-fore ever pertinent and focus on praxis. The latter is a term highly ecologi-cal as well as pedagogical. Timothy Morton in his book *The Ecological Thought* defines the ecological praxis as a fundamentally Aristotelian contemplative act because '[r]eframing our world, our problems, and ourselves is part of the ecological project. This is what praxis means – action that is thoughtful and thought that is active' (2010:8–9). This is linked to pedagogy because it entails the contemplative configurations of speculative (and therefore academic) practice coming in effect for future people (Guattari, 2001:76).

The ecological and the pedagogical praxis go – or ought to go – hand in hand. Prolific and controversial Brazilian pedagogist Paulo Freire in the chapter that focuses on the importance of dialogue in education and life in his seminal book *The Pedagogy of the Oppressed* defines praxis as tool for transforming the world, a synthesis of work and word, and action and reflection (2017:60). He explains the risks of losing any of these constitutive elements that wither leads to no action (verbalism) or an impossible dialogue (activism) (2017:60–61). Freire also emphasises the role of (true) word in the pedagogical act in times of crisis when silence is valued only when contemplative (and therefore within the world) and not when it 'signifies contempt for the world and flight from it in a type of "historical schizophrenia"' (2017:61). This is important to note here and will be further discussed in Synapsis II because Freire adds this as a note to his statement that 'human beings are not built merely in silence, but in word, work, in action-reflection' (2017:61) and therefore in praxis.

There are two significant points to take forward from Freire's work, apart from the obvious phenomenological and dialectic (or dialogical) treatise,[3] which is not of pertinence here. The first point is the notion of transformation (of the world) as part of the pedagogical act, which entails critical thinking 'which perceives reality as process . . . rather than static entity – thinking which does not separate itself from action, but constantly immerses itself in temporality' 2017:65) – a humanisation. This implies a becoming.[4] The second important point Freire – quite subtly – makes here is the problematic recall of historicity. Both points are picked up by Petra Hroch in her essay 'Deleuze, Guattari and Environmental Pedagogy and Politics' (2014), which is particularly pertinent here because of its rhizomatic, geophilosophic approach. Hroch advocates for an education for (my emphasis) 'people-in-becoming' and refers to the contingencies of the zeitgeist as part of critical thinking that (ought to) lead pedagogical transformation. She adds that 'the philosophical challenge for us today is not to seek to return to an origin, a point of departure, a philosophical home to which we may (or may never) have belonged (and to which we certainly no longer belong)' (2014:52–53). This is not a polemic to a radical pedagogy. On the contrary it recentres the now-future as anchor for returning to root and remaining contemporary.

Playing Dostoyevsky's Idiot: "But-why?"

Education has been mundanely seen for a long time by institutions, peda-gogists, and most crucially learners themselves as the foundation pillar of inquisition and acquisition of information, knowledge, or skill – namely intelligence – and this is the home we certainly no longer belong to. This is what Paulo Freire's 'banking concept in education' (2017:45) alludes to. Freire distinctively notes that 'education is suffering from narration sickness . . . it becomes an act of depositing' (2017:44–45). Again, and very much against his phenomenological treatise, Freire distinguishes the dissemination of information (banking) to knowledge instilling (problem-posing) noting that the latter 'emerges only through invention and re-invention, through the restless, impatient, continuing, hopeful enquiry human beings pursue in the world, with the world, and with each other' (2017:45), a becoming human with the world and not a 'better "fit" for the world' (2017:49). Although Freire makes a very clear statement that his pedagogy is humanist (and libertarian) (2017:28), it is evident that it can now also be read as ecological and therefore with post-human (Braidotti, 2013) and nomadic (Braidotti, 2006) ramifica-tions, because the human in education is not the individualistic 'I' but an eco-logical entity (Braidotti, 2006:41). We can see this clearly when Freire calls the libertarian pedagogist a 'teacher-of-the-students' (2017:53).

To become educated has been widely assigned to humans by humans almost as autotelic quality, what Freire calls 'the vocation of becoming more fully human' (2017:40). It presupposes one autopoietic threshold that educators and learners tend to keep being oblivious to, which is the learning itself as a praxis of enabling oneself to learn how to learn. Just like the ques-tion of humanism, posed by Freire in the context of pedagogy, the question of education is ancient and current, mature, and nascent – immanent. Edu-cation remains achronous and relevant beyond the à la mode yet reflective of the zeitgeist (a critical thinking praxis) and has received philosophical treatise and practical advancement since the classical times. If we agree with Beatriz Colomina and Mark Wigley and their seminal book, *Are We Human?* that we do not merely learn how to 'invent tools' (2019:51) but are able to define our evolution by designing and as David R. Cole notes enhancing those tools (Cole, 2021), we may open a Pandora's Box full of maladies and panaceas; agents that may allow by critical reflection (a peda-gogical act) a practically and broadly beneficial redefinition of contempo-rary learning and living – an ecological act.

This book attempts such redefinition, particularly in the context of adult formal and lifelong education, most prominently drawing from emergent learning approaches and observations in academic practice that involves praxis (vocation-led curricula) and everyday life. Pedagogy (as per etymology and close definition) has been primarily concerned with principles of education as schooling, and less (despite etymology) about leading the learner and the learning praxis that is beyond the planned currere and more about the lived experience (Aoki, 2005). Its manifestation in published matter is almost exclusive of poetic theorisations for learning and teaching that concern adult life, and therefore the population de droit able to make learning decisions and present ownership of their learning capacities. This exclusion, almost an unobserved lacuna in the weave of shaping human evolution by design, is complemented by either warped eclecticism in over politicising and policing recent theories of pedagogy that otherwise seem to make a valid point on education or relentless fixations to disciplinary focused approaches. Both fail to make a clear distinction between pedagogy and curriculum and address perhaps the most important aspect of education as critique (pedagogy) rather than analysis. What we (educators and most importantly learners) are left with are a 'market ideology' (Mayo, 2020: 35), textbooks, policy indexes and subject-specific instructions that often lack pragmatism and are devoid of diversity or idiosyncrasy and lead to an oppressive and therefore risky prescription (Freire, 2017:21).

This book consciously does not seek to postulate or populate such approaches. It instead turns to non-contemporary literary theory, memoirs, and post-theory tangent to education to address problems and propose paradigm shifts that can fuel praxis as pedagogical and ecological thought and act with-the-world. It is essential that we now set some baseline assumptions that will form the foundations for approaching such multifaceted and critical subject as education as pedagogy and culture in an ecological context. We also need to need to establish a clear distinction between education and erudition. The latter is the focus of this book and entails constitutional values that may need to be challenged or reappreciated and which has cultural and ecological merits. Education, in the context of this book, is stressed as performative infrastructure of curricula that cares for the systemic and institutionalised merit of intelligence, which is nevertheless a social, political, and economic (therefore also ecological) praxis within and for the lived world. Both ought to be constitutional elements of pedagogy and ecology.

Ecosystemic Idiocracy

We have been proving our ecological astigmatism for more than 4,000 years and this is fundamentally a problem of education as well as erudition. We will be discussing the definitions and distinctions of these terms in Part 2. From the hired slave (a pedagogue) to the academy master and hereafter the precarious worker, educators have had the capacity to shape and define the Anthropos of the next generation being themselves a generation behind. This innate discrepancy of education has become even more so notable now, in the age of Supermodernity (Auge, 2009) because of the learning modalities chiasm between the learner and the educator. In other words, educators have become systemically and experientially disabled to catch up with two fundamental things: (i) to follow the learners in their pattern of learning which is increasingly different to the teacher's pattern of learning as learner, and (ii) to ensure the resilience and relativity that come with what is taught and learnt and how, and the way this will remain applicable and useful in the future. The latter is starting to emerge as a severe impediment for formal education that is becoming progressively less associated with erudition and cultivation because it fails to acknowledge the learner's consciousness.

We are dazed to read that 'around 85% of the jobs that today's learners will be doing in 2030 haven't been invented yet' (Institute for the Future for DELL Technologies, 2017:14). We should perhaps start realising even more so shockingly, that radiologists for instance (a popular University study choice) will soon be made extinct by AI and that 'by 2045 a non-biological intelligence[?] will have rendered our human intelligence obsolete' Jean-Michel Besnier debates with Laurent Alexandre in *Do Robots Make Love? From AI to Immortality* (2018:84). Besnier makes another statement in *Do Robots Make Love?* that for me summarises the past, present and perhaps not so luminous future of ours: 'the indices of our species and by which our species alone can claim to have a history' are technology as tools (practicum) and language as words (theoria) by reference to Plato in Protagoras (2018:21) and Aristotle in Nichomachean Ethics (Roochnik, 2009:69). Tools and words have been the sword and shield of education and erudition, yet we must emphasise that tools themselves by default make our bodies 'qua human' (Stigler, 1998:152). We must also question respectively what the words themselves can do in an access-to-data-driven learning world. It is the value of technology and language assigned to learnt capacities that have so far determined income and capital and not the 'differences in mental ability' as Alexandre and Besnier note (2018:103–104). Intelligence therefore acquires a conflicting relationship with education as we move from meritocracy to mediocracy, and perhaps Idiocracy as depicted in the popular 2006 film by Mike Judge – when intelligence becomes ominously detached from education (Judge, 2006).

This means in the context of our discussion on education that there has been investment on the value of education in analogy to employability or perhaps infrastructural accommodation of vocational training. We must perhaps invest instead on the training of the skill of attitude (critical thinking of praxis) towards learning to learn and building autonomy and resilience in learning through life (Nicol and Pilling, 2000:6) for both the learner and the educator, considering both as constitutional elements of an ecology called erudition. This makes us come back to Aoki's concept of lived curriculum and the notion of 'indwelling between two curriculum worlds' (2005:159) in the story of Miss O – the zone between the planned and the lived. Aoki describes the teacher as the entity that oscillates between the two and can reach a momentum of necropolitical self-reflection as to question, 'Survive? What For?' (2005:163) in 'a mode that could be oppressive and depressive, marked by despair and hopelessness, and at other times, challenging and stimulating, evoking hopefulness for venturing forth' (Aoki, 2005:162). This tensionality is an aftermath of the precarious dialectic that the curriculum awaiting implementation and the lived experience create. Learners are now also in the limbo of the zone in between planned and lived curricula. In Synapsis III, we will define two distinctive profiles of such.

An Illness of One's Own

The stagnate waters of adult education from a systemic and pedagogical point of view in advanced capitalist societies have been suffering from an 'exhaustion of the future' and a 'culture that is merely preserved as no culture at all' notes Mark Fisher by reference to T.S. Elliot on the definition of capitalism in his seminal book Capitalist Realism (2009:3). Even more so prominently he continues to define the capitalism state (our real country of residence as people) – just like education – as 'a strange hybrid of the ultramodern and the archaic' (2009:6). We must admit that the need to remain relevant in the machines that sustain our capitalistic de-territorialised yet situated homelands, we accept this hybrid as a chronic condition that we learn to live with, and which dominates education and in most conservative cases demonises erudition. We have allowed as Fisher notes a generation to become ill by reflexive impotence and disengagement that often translates into polarised extremes of aboulia or neurasthenic burnouts. Six in ten (63%) students say that they feel levels of stress that interfere with their day to day lives. Additionally, 77% of all students report that they have 'a fear of failure' according to YouGov reports (Aronin and Smith, 2016). Yet, we privatise each of them in an atomistic manner, ignoring the inherent pathology of a population that enters adulthood unassumingly yet ever so coolly affording the illness. Let us contemplate again that new illnesses in crisis are born from the contemporary system itself, which not only does not have the tool enhancement tactics to eliminate them but shamefully sustains them.

Fisher hits the nail on the head when he notes that 'what we deal in the classroom is a generation born into that ahistorical, anti-mnemonic blip culture . . . [that suffers from] post-lexia' (2009:25). Indeed, we live in the 'post-era' when all is inscribed in and prescribed by technological innovation (Ihde, 1993) and this era is fundamentally capitalistic. As Deleuze and Guattari mention in Anti-Oedipus, 'capitalism is profoundly illiterate' (1983:240). This means that we have lost half of what defines our species as anthropotis (humanity). We lost the words that would make us able to keep carrying (and enhancing) the tools. We are helpless Prometheans holding a fire we were so preoccupied of sustaining we do not know how to extinguish. We have been already and long ago destined to become cyborgs: post-human ahistorical creatures moving towards another extinction in the dawn of the post-Anthropocene. This late capitalist era we live in is 'realer than the real' (Massumi, 1987) and we, educators, either passively reproduce or faintly coup against the problem. We as such mirror our learners and oscillate between aboulia and burnout, making learning itself (and education) an illness of one's own, manifesting as stress, debt, and excruciating tedium. Let this not be a morbid obituary of education, but a pedagogical act of reflective criticism against pedagogy and its situatedness in the current educational, economic, social, and therefore ecological affairs.

A Tale of Viruses and Nerves

When Byung-Chul Han wrote the book *The Burnout Society* (2015), he was attributing the pathologies of learning and living stemming from late capitalism to the genome of a generation of learners (and teachers) who are not immunologically but instead neurologically suffering. He writes: "[f]rom a pathological standpoint, the incipient twenty-first century is determined neither by bacteria nor by viruses, but by neurons" (2015:1). Five years later, Han is not necessarily proven wrong because of the global COVID-19 pandemic. On the contrary, his statement rationalises very eloquently the extent of the life learning skills issue (deeply an issue of erudition) that shaped the global cartography of the pandemic. A pandemic in an age of medical and technological immediacy – where communication is oversaturated and access to information is a commons – is a problem of assessment, appraisal, and personal and communal responsibility. At the rise of 2020 we were blissfully arrogant (mainly ahistorical rather than ignorant) against a wide immunological failure and at the same time already neurologically ill, burnt-out, and impotent of reflex. We can read this crisis labelled as immunological is being a pedagogical and ecological event, particularly as it features evenly together in the news with climate emergency. It is also no coincidence that we are using the term climate literacy and digital literacy ever so often in education and curricula that are linked to vocational subjects (prescribed) and perhaps we can consider both as constitutive elements of the education-to-come.

Mark Fisher's reflexive impotence and Han's profound boredom are each other's simulacra, so are digital and climate literacy in education and prescribed curricula. We must not think of either as thunder that struck humanity on the 1st dawn of any year or century. We must furthermore not assume that the infrastructural mania to address these in the currere is a millennial custom. It is rooted in modernity and the era of transition of professional pursuit of working class from labour to civil service. Portuguese poet Fernando Pessoa dedicates his fragmented memoirs (from 1912 until his death in 1935) in the posthumously published *Book of Disquiet* (2010) to tedium, which we will examine extensively in terms of its pedagogical content and the definition of erudition in the next part (Synapsis I) of this book. Anson Rabinbach presents almost a clinical philosophy of the same subject in the chapter of *The Human Motor* called 'Mental Fatigue, Neurasthenia and Civilisation' (1992:146–178). Rabinbach agrees with Han and Fisher that modern and late-capitalistic worlds elevate achievement as ultimate manifestation of fulfilment and success. This is often linked to academic progression or professional development and which under the excessive demands of civilisation (and tool-enhancement) leads to other polarised maladies such as extreme disquiet and subsequently no habitation to will (aboulia) (156–161). This malady is a projection of another malady we will discuss: the loss of desire in affective life and the 'law of the least effort' not anymore as economy (in the age of labour) but as asthenia (in the age of achievement) (Rabinbach, 1992:172–176), and all link to the malady we call reality.

It becomes apparent therefore that education as erudition is now facing apart from annihilation a great paradox. It requires strong foundations of training (practicum) to treat intellectual fatigue and experiential poverty and concomitantly foster and disseminate words (theoria) to fight aboulia and political passivity. This book attempts to address this paradox with a view to interrogate and make propositions for acting as praxis. It will follow a rhizomorphous meta-structure growing Deleuze and Guattari's 'rhizome' from *A Thousand Plateaus* into a radical synaptic system (1987:17). In the next Part (which is Synapsis I) we will start addressing the role of theory in the process of establishing learning principles in response to the above and we will explore a network of intergrowing attributes that define education and erudition with a focus on the latter as cultural ecology of learning. The following chapter (Synapsis II) will offer a treatise of the role of desire in the cartography of the learning process and the importance of networks and machines as agents of critical pedagogy that happens with-the-world, for people-in-becoming reading Fernand Deligny's *The Arachnean* (2015) and offering therefore a posthuman perspective. Synapsis III unfolds the characteristics of a learners' network as a-people-to-come and presents reflecting on academic practice as case study two scholars' profiles as constitutive elements of a pedagogy: the maverick and the temperate. In the final chapter book returns to Part 1 (root) debating a new index of adult education as erudition synthesising Synapses I, II, and III.

Notes

1 See www.bbc.co.uk/programmes/p005k2yw and www.bbc.co.uk/programmes/articles/2j6SZdsHLrnNd8nGFB5f5S/20-things-from-the-year-2000-that-will-make-you-feel-nostalgic
2 paraphrasing Alain de Botton in *The School of Life* (2020:22).
3 Freire consistently cites Husserl and Merleau-Ponty and Hegel in his work, alongside Marx and Hegel.
4 Earlier in the book Freire assigns this becoming to 'problem-posing education [which] affirms men and women as beings in the process of becoming' (2017:57) and which we will discuss in the following parts of this book.

References

Alexandre, L. and Besnier, J. M. (2018) *Do Robots Make Love? From AI to Immortality*. London: Octopus Books.
Aoki, Ted T. (2005) *Curriculum in a New Key: The Collected Works of Ted T. Aoki*. Ed by W. F. Pinar and R. L. Irwin. Mahwah, NJ: Lawrence Erlbaum.
Aronin, S. and Smith, M. (2016) 'Stress and anxiety are making day to day life difficult for hundreds of thousands of students' *YouGov*, 9 August 2016. https://yougov.co.uk/topics/lifestyle/articles-reports/2016/08/09/quarter-britains-students-are-afflicted-mental-hea. (Last accessed 8 July 2020).
Auge, M. (2009) *Non-places: Introduction to an Anthropology of Supermodernity: An Introduction to Supermodernity*. London: Verso.
Braidotti, R. (2006) *Transpositions: On Nomadic Ethics*. Cambridge: Polity.
Braidotti, R. (2013) *The Posthuman*. Cambridge: Polity.
Cole, D. R. (2021) *Education, the Anthropocene, and Deleuze/Guattari*. Leiden and Boston: Brill.
Colomina, B. and Wigley, M. (2019) *Are We Human? Notes on an Archaeology of Design*. Zürich: Lars Müller.
Conley, V. A. (2009) 'Artists or "Little Soldiers?" Félix Guattari's Ecological Paradigms' in B. Herzongenrath (ed.), *Deleuze | Guattari & Ecology*. Basingstoke: Palgrave Macmillan.
de Botton, A. (2020) *The School of Life: An Emotional Education*. London: Penguin.
Deleuze, G. and Guattari, F. (1983) *Anti-Oedipus; Capitalism and Schizophrenia*. Trans by R. Hurley, M. Seem, and H. R. Lane. Minneapolis: University of Minnesota Press.
Deleuze, G. and Guattari, F. (1987) *A Thousand Plateaus; Capitalism and Schizophrenia*. Trans by B. Massumi. Minneapolis and London: University of Minnesota Press.
Deligny, F. (2015) *The Arachnean and Other Texts*. Minneapolis: Univocal Publishing.
Fisher, M. (2009) *Capitalism Realism; Is There No Alternative?* Winchester: Zero Books.
Freire, P. (2017) [1970] *Pedagogy of the Oppressed*. Trans by Myra Bergman Ramos. London: Penguin.

Frichot, H. (2018) *Creative Ecologies, Theorising the Practice of Architecture*. London: Bloomsbury.

Guattari, F. (2001) [1989] *The Three Ecologies*. Trans by I. Pintar and P. Sutton. London and New Brunswick, NJ: Athlone Press.

Han, B.-C. (2015) *The Burnout Society*. Stanford, CA: Stanford University Press.

Hroch, P. (2014) 'Deleuze, Guattari and Environmental Pedagogy and Politics: Ritournelles for a Planet-yet-To-Come' in M. Carlin and J. Wallin (eds.), *Deleuze and Guattari, Politics and Education: For a People-Yet-to-Come*. London: Bloomsbury. 49–75.

Ihde, D. (1993) *Postphenomenology: Essays in the Postmodern Context*. Evanston, IL: The Northwestern University Press.

Institute for the Future (IFTF) for DELL Technologies (2017) *The Next Era of Human | Machine Partnerships; Emerging Technologies' Impact on Society & Work in 2030*. www.delltechnologies.com/en-gb/perspectives/the-next-era-of-human-machine-partnerships/. (Last accessed 8 July 2020).

Judge, M. (2006) *Idiocracy*. Twentieth Century Fox.

Massumi, B. (1987) 'Realer Than Real: The Simulacrum According to Deleuze and Guattari' in *Copyright*, Vol. 1. (archived) www.anu.edu.au/hrc/first_and_last/works/realer.html. (Last accessed 8 July 2020).

Mayo, (2020) [2009] 'Critical Pedagogy in Difficult Times' in Sheila L. Macrine (ed.), *Critical Pedagogy in Uncertain Times: Hope and Possibilities*. 2nd ed. Cham: Palgrave Macmillan. 33–43.

Morton, T. (2010) *The Ecological Thought*. Cambridge: Harvard University Press.

Nicol, D. and Pilling, S. (2000) *Changing Architectural Education: Towards a New Professionalism*. London: SPON Press.

Pessoa, F. (2010) *The Book of Disquiet*. Trans by Margaret Jull Costa. London: Serpent's Tail.

Rabinbach, R. (1992) *The Human Motor: Energy, Fatigue, and Origins of Modernity*. Berkley: University of California Press.

Roochnik, D. (2009) 'What is Theoria? Nicomachean Ethics Book 10.7–8' in *Classical Philology*, Vol. 104 (1). The University of Chicago Press. 69–82. doi:10.1086/603572. (Last accessed 8 July 2020).

Stigler, B. (1998) *Technics and Time, 1: The Fault of Epimetheus*. Redwood City, CA: Stanford University Press.

Wallin, J. (2014) 'Education Needs to Get a Grip of Life' in M. Carlin and J. Wallin (eds.), *Deleuze and Guattari, Politics and Education: For a People-Yet-to-Come*. London: Bloomsbury. 118–139.

Part 2

Synapsis I

Aristotle, Pessoa, and the Missing Cultures: Erudition

'pedagogy is never innocent'

(Giroux, 2020:87)

In the previous Part (Tuber) we discussed an archetypal affiliation of the notion of education to intelligence, and the possibility of moving towards an intelligence that is forensic and therefore ecological – a pedagogy. The critical term curriculum was also introduced as constitutional element of education and therefore tool for pedagogical transformation once in the in between space of planning for and living the event of learning. The latter was stressed as praxis of pedagogy – an ecology of contemplative thought and critical, reflective action. This Part (Synapsis I) will create a space to synthesise learner, educator and learning into a pedagogical ecology through the concept of desire and approaching currere as a verb and there-fore a praxis towards an affective pedagogy. To do so, the synthesis form-ing Synapsis I will entail literary criticism, philosophy, and pedagogical references, as relevant to establish key definitions of education (Aristotle) and erudition (Portuguese poet Fernando Pessoa). It furthermore offers a conjunctive synthesis and critical and reflective analogy of the key triads offered by Aristotle and Pessoa for education and erudition respectively. It sees those triads as radicles of thought that can potentially create an ever so relevant cartography of pedagogy, each expanding eclectically upon ethical, ecological, and cultural ramifications of the event of learning, which will be mapped out in the next Part of this book (Synapsis II).

Let us return to the philosopher who defined education as linked to intel-ligence and continues to affect pedagogical thought – Aristotle. From his *Ethics and Politics* (Burnet, 1968), we can extract that Aristotle's education is a 'cultivation of the mind' (Collins, 1990:73) toward the common good – a democratic rather than a democratised curriculum, with a strong ethical

DOI: 10.4324/9781003220619-3

and therefore symptomatically ecological core. As Robb notes, 'character training in Aristotle's scheme of education takes precedence over all other immediate objectives of the school' (Robb, 1943:207). One cannot help and wonder throughout the genealogies of formal policy in education as well as developments in pedagogy in the western and westernised world, how we led ourselves to consider that 'when knowledge is dead, they call it the academy' (Bernard quoted in Preciado, 2019:50) and to deliver an over-professionalised education and a 'University system [that] is training people for outdated jobs' (Alexandre and Besnier, 2018:116). The School in its constitutive counterparts must stand on giant's shoulders; on principles of virtue as well as critical thinking, collaborative poesis and holistic praxis (Psarologaki, 2020:28). It is indeed a democratic and libertarian praxis, a praxis of Aristotelian virtue, and Freire's pedagogy of hope (Freire, 2021). As we are examining the problematics of vocational curricula and the capitalistic marketisation of pedagogical trends, particularly in Higher Education, it is worth looking at a key term of Aristotle, beyond but also through his definition of education as the civilisation of παιδεία (the shape of good character) (Tachibana, 2012). This term I consider constitutive to pedagogy futures, is scholē (σχολή), and which according to Aristotle is integrative to human existence – a contemplative down time and not leisure, a ceremonial closure, a timeless Sunday. This is not however a complete switch-off, but a creative acedia.

Schole as leisure lies 'outside of work and outside of inactivity' says Byung-Chul Han in the book *The Scent of Time* (2017), and 'thinking as theorein, as the contemplative consideration of truth is based on [this] . . . (bios theoretikos)[1]' (2017:87). I would like to further assign schole not only to philosophein but also to constitutive characteristics in all kinds of Aristotelian life particularly as education is becoming professionalised and because the democratic character of (self-)improvement for the common good (virtue); to hedone of and in a-scholia (work) as well as the desire towards bios politikos (the commons). We will use schole here as study – time spend contemplatively on improvement and transformation that complements and therefore within a transformed pedagogy can be seen as ethical contribution to work (a-scholia). It is only by praxis of schole one can aspire to have an a-scholia – a profession – and a democratic citizenship. It means one is becoming available, and 'lingering, [and] presupposes a gathering of the senses' (Han, 2017:87). The latter is a deeply pedagogical concept. Inna Semetsky returns to Floyd Merrell to define what a 'bodymind' in learning is – 'an integrated mode of thought [therefore praxis, my emphasis here] that enables one to live to learn, and to learn to live' (2013:80), and this says Semetsky is affective, actualised in practical life (Aristotle's prakta) but 'from the depths of the collective unconscious' (2013:84). Like Semetsky with Merrell, David R. Cole draws from Glasser's Choice Theory to determine the idiosyncrasy of affective literacy (Cole, 2013:94–111) based on the scholar's needs, the latter being survival, love, belonging and acceptance, freedom, fun and learning, among others (Glasser, 1998:5). This puts affect in the centre not only learning but the ecology of pedagogy.

Scholē and Tedium

I would like to draw here an important analogy in the context of mapping out a pedagogy of desire and erudition, that would allow the exploration of the contemporary positioning of education against its maladies with a view of a future transformation because of them and not despite of or against them. This is because as noted earlier, the illness that is new during an institutional crisis belongs to the institution itself and becomes its reality, its suggestive matter, its pulp of things.[2] This analogy is between Aristotle's schole as examined extensively by Byung-Chul Han in the book *The Scent of Time* (2017) and the notion of the inertia of 'tedium' in Fernando Pessoa's The Book of Disquiet (2010):

> Expressed as direct sensation, it is as if the drawbridge over the moat around the soul's castle had been pulled up, leaving us with but one power, that of gazing impotently out at surrounding lands never again to set foot there. We are isolated within ourselves from ourselves, an isolation in which what separates us is as stagnant in us, a pool of dirty water surrounding our inability to understand.
>
> (118–119)

> We were born into a state if anguish, both metaphysical and moral, and of political disquiet.
>
> (206)

Pessoa's tedium is the evil twin and the dark precursor, a 'quasi-homonym' (Deleuze, 1994:122) to Aristotle's schole. It is 'the lack of a mythology' (Pessoa, 2010:120), the lack of an imagination. Whilst schole is leisure by contemplation that critically contributes by ethical praxis to St Augustine's vita activa (vita contemplativa), tedium manifests as the spiral of idleness and inability to affect and become affected, an esoteric incapacity to become human – 'a backward leaning, inhumane tendency' (Greene and Macrine, 2009:82), Dewey's 'anaesthetic' (Dewey, 1931:40) and Camy's start of The Plague 'where everyone is bored and devotes himself to cultivating habits' (1984:4), unable to 'imagine not what is necessarily probable or predictable, but what may be conceived as possible' (Greene and Macrine, 2009:82) and therefore to become future.

To address this, let us go back to the notion of contemplating. Byung-Chul Han in his chapter 'Profound Boredom', in the book *Burnout Society* (2015), notably associates tedium with the loss of contemplative attention and the ability to immerse oneself, which ontologically presupposes a loss of culture and pedagogy. This is primarily because 'culture presumes an environment in which deep attention is possible' (Han, 2015:13). Instead, we experience life in a condition of hyperattention . . . a rash change of focus between different tasks, sources of information. and processes' (Han, 2015:13), which leaves no clearly defined contemplative interval to affirm a life. 'Human life is impoverished when all forms of in-between are removed from it' (Han, 2017:38). There is no space left for the contemplative praxis of education that is embedded in common life and culture, a lingering in between the bios theoretikos and the bios politikos. This book defines the emancipatory effect of this lingering as erudition, which is by meaning associated broadly with scholarship. We will focus on the association therefore of erudition with the Aristotelian schole, based on its critical delineation extracted from Pessoa in the *Book of Disquiet* (2010). He notes that '[t]here is an erudition of knowledge, which is what we usually mean by "erudition", and there is an erudition of understanding, which is what we call culture' (2010:77).

Culture, the cultivation of oneself into an ecological and ethical collective, is of course the manifestation of education as erudition, as emancipation. Alfred North Whitehead at the start of his book *The Aims of Education and Other Essays* (1929) distinguishes the notion of education as reception and digestion of knowledge [Freire's concept of 'banking' (Freire, 2017:45) in education] from erudition noting the affective character and praxis of critical thinking as constitutive qualities of a culture. He says 'culture is activity of thought and receptiveness to beauty and human feeling. Scraps of information have nothing to do with it' (Whitehead, 1929:1). 'But there is also an erudition of sensibility' (2010:77) Pessoa says and he associates this with an emancipation in living by travelling, which we can associate with a nomadism. This is important because Pessoa – in his fragmented memoir – implies a deeply ecological and pedagogical statement. Tedium hinders the cultural aspect of education, defined as erudition. It prevents the becoming of a culture and therefore creates a hindsight of possible futures and of any transformation avenue. Furthermore, erudition, unlike education per se, is a constitutive term of culture, a critical term of emancipatory life and implies a perlocutionary act – praxis aiming for evolutionary (and revolutionary) change. Erudition is enabled by schole and deep contemplative immersion in between structured learning and experiencing; by critical pedagogy – by ecological and ethical praxis. It is education by affective and reflective action and by sensibility.

The Impotent Scholar[3]

Tedium and the loss of the ability to contemplate has been widely associated with the phenomenon of boredom brought by modernity. In the chapter 'Pedagogy of Seeing' in *Burnout Society* (2015) Byung Chul Han says we are transforming into 'autistic performing machines' (Han, 2015:23). We are trained to and training others to be afraid of doing nothing and be bored leading each other into tedium. This phenomenon did not appear as an ecosystemic malady recently. On the contrary, there is evidence it has been cultivated for a long time – almost as if what we call civilisation gave birth to it – and deteriorated by capitalism and the neurologically ill generation of post-2000. Since modernity and the industrial revolution, mental and physical stress particularly in young people who are in education has been studied as a social and pedagogical phenomenon consistently in central Europe and most prominently Germany. Anson Rabinbach in his book *The Human Motor* creates a genealogy of boredom, anxiety and mental fatigue as related to what was called neurasthenia, 'the most extreme mental fatigue' (Rabinbach, 1992:153). He associates the latter to lassitude by intellectual exhaustion; a phenomenon that seems to have been observed in highly performing learners (Rabinbach, 1992:147). This, he implies, can lead to loss of culture and pedagogy – and therefore loss of erudition as defined here. He also notes that 'contemporary humanity does not have sufficient capacity for adaptability, to tolerate the increase and expansion of life work without injury' (1992:151) and interestingly assigns this malady manifesting as 'extreme disquiet' (1992:156) to the scholar's brain who suffers a fatigue anaesthesia/amnesia and 'is too tired to remember to be tired' (1992:161). It seems that this kind of stress has now become an assigned illness for our generation of educators (McFarlane, 2005) and most prominently learners in schooling and particularly in post-compulsory and higher education, at least in the UK. This kind of disquiet is different to Pessoa's disquiet. The latter is a condition of critical thinking and of questioning life through experiencing, of knowledge, of culture and of sensibility; evidence of an erudition and schole.

We are discussing here the maladies of a neurologically (and since COVID-19 also immunologically) suffering age that is burnt out and proudly demonstrating loss of creative and contemplative attention (Han, 2015:13). Contemporary learners are in principle tool-savvy but ahistorical and struggle to approach and to experience education as lifelong emotional (and intellectual) need – an erudition – even when the latter is apparently accessible. This is perhaps because of limited affective capacity to immerse themselves in schole; in study and critical thinking by contemplation. K-punk author Mark Fisher in his book *Capitalism Realism* calls this a 'reflexive impotence' (Fisher, 2009). Fisher defines this impotence as an ontological inability to imagine new ways of being and tendency to settle for a future that never comes. He stresses that we ask how come and so many young people are ill from what he sees as privatised stress. Talking about learners he says, 'they know things are bad, but more than that, they know they can't do anything about it' (Fisher, 2009:25). It seems that the will has to be educated itself to endure the strains of civilisation and desire is a primitive form of affective drive for life. When power of desire is negative, will is weak, and the need for education (as erudition) is suppressed creating an 'inferior student whose impaired performance [is] a consequence of the exhaustion' (Rabinbach, 1992:152). Fisher's reflexive impotence is Pessoa's tedium. It is not boredom, and it is not leisure. It lacks schole and contemplative immersion in critical thinking therefore being incompatible with Freire's notion of the 'historical and ontological vocation of becoming more fully human' (Freire, 2017:40) – Pessoa's nomadic 'erudition' (2010:77). This will be further discussed in Part 3 (Synapsis II) and Part 4 (Synapsis III) of this book as related to networks of desire and a people-in-becoming respectively, through Whitehead's tripartite classification of the rhythm of education; romance, precision, and generalisation (synthesis).

Desire to Defer?

We have moved from acceleration – which was the fundamental quality and aim of modernity – to deferral as Paul Beatriz Preciado notes (2019:62–63) bringing a up a common thread with Byung Chul Han in the phenomenon of the mobile game and social media compatible application called Candy Crush Saga. Preciado calls Candy Crush Saga 'a discipline of the soul, an immaterial prison proposing a constant deferral of desire and action . . . not to teach the users anything, but to capture the totality of their cognitive capacities' (Preciado, 2019:62–63). It is true that 'contemporary technology subjects us to signs and signifiers that are . . . numerous and insistent, demanding faster and faster behavioural reaction' (Alexandre and Besnier, 2018:136). This is not however a statement of technophobic interpretation in response to current affairs. It is more of an ecological thought – a question of what we desire to be immersed in. Immersion says Timothy Morton is an ecological concept because it implies an enveloping environment – an ambience (Morton, 2018:196). Immersion can also be considered a fundamentally pedagogical concept, and we can turn to Rabinbach for that, who relates immersion with an affective state of pre-conscious regression from will (that normally overrules desire) to desire where the latter 'asserts its power unchallenged' (Rabinbach, 1992:165). He also sees aboulia (tedium) due to mental exhaustion as a wrongful application of the 'law of least effort' (1992:172) and the economy and 'avoidance of labour' (1992:176), what we contemporarily call naively procrastination. The most important point in Rabinbach's thought is that he sees desire pedagogically and that he creates an ecology of education-born illness that can be addressed eco-systemically within the context that creates it, and when such psychological or pedagogical insight can be tailored to the environment within which it grows (1992:172) the latter can be transformed.

When Rabinbach talks about immersion and contemplation however, he makes a distinction. He sees the first as an affective state like religious ecstasy driven by desire and therefore primitive and preconscious. He then associates the latter with a quality that is ontologically and biologically (ecologically as well) humane, but then so is neurasthenia on the other side of the spectrum (in terms of the notion of being within a condition). Han highlights the cultural ramifications of acceleration (of modernity and what-ever followed thereafter):

> the sequence of cuts or events is intensified to the point of hysteria, and takes hold of all areas of life . . . the senses are constantly provided with nee or drastic perceptions. Point-time does not permit any contempla-tive lingering.

> (Han, 2017:18)

This is crucial for contemplation (and immersion) to happen, and conse-quently for education and erudition. The question is whether the ability to contemplate is a lost culture or not at all a distinctively humane capacity. I would like at this point to associate the praxis of critical thought that is constitutive to learning and erudition by association to lingering as immer-sion and contemplation with responsibility and compassion. Perhaps there is no forgotten dimension or quality in contemplation because we – as humanity as we know of it – never succeeded in ecosystemically acquir-ing it. We just failed to develop it and now we are battling two dragons in the den: individual and collective responsibility, which we thought we had but we do not, and it manifests in many aspects of society, economy and of course education. Culture and contemplation can make us ethical humans and societies, and each is potentially a matter of erudition. Both also entail individual and collective responsibility. This is important because within the context of a highly consumeristic world the notion of erudition for the common good, and therefore education as part of the bios politikos through the responsibility worn by the individual, has been replaced by the opportu-nity to access a privatised consumption (Mayo, 2020:35–36). We will return to this in Part 4 (Synapsis III) when we discuss democracy and citizenship in a learning people.

Culture is the historical and anthropological dimension in ourselves that extends beyond us as organisms and as contributors within an ecosystem and within a society, and economy. It connects us with others and the environment – it is our ecological DNA (Morton, 2018:197). Currently and for some time now, this is casually, habitually, and conveniently possible via our tool enhancement. We consistently live (not just use) with mobile devices that connect with the world but also notably separate us from the environment and from others. At the same time, they do not hold the inherent value of objecthood; they are consumables. We are not consciously and compassionately situated in place. According to Han this is because through them we live in instantaneity, where everything is here, and becomes available (Han, 2017:39) and one can literally zap (or scroll) through the world without moving but their fingertips (sometimes the only thing it takes is a 'Hey Siri' or 'Alexa'). This is not new and again we should not demonise our tools. Our tools-enhancement is integral part of educative aspect of human life (Cole, 2021) have been shaping us into what and who we are, it has defined our pulp. We might, however, question the processes and contexts that have led us to ontologically reach a point where we no more question of the origins of things as part of our everyday life, by spending time in effectively not trying to achieve anything but a contemplative praxis, and which has led us to abandon schole altogether. The answer comes from Bell Hooks in *Teaching Community: A Pedagogy of Hope*, quoting Steven Blazer: it is 'to simply ground education with experience' (Hooks, 2003:182) to assume 'social responsibility and compassion' (Giroux, 2020:48). This is a praxis of human transformation, demonstrating collectively and individually pedagogical and ecological ethos because it creates and sustains the 'connective tissue that enables students to raise issues about the consequences of their actions' (Giroux, 2020:224).

To Currere

As noted earlier, we can agree with Han that today's experience is characterised by the fact that it is very poor in transitions' (Han, 2017:37). Furthermore, there is no space in between the distinctive points of such and this hinders contemplative learning – what we defined as erudition by culture and by sensibility. This, as discussed, is a pedagogical issue with ecological ramifications. To address this, we will go back to what pedagogy can mean in a reality of such malady. Pedagogy has often been associated with 'philosophy of education, educational theory, or pedagogy of practice' (Semetsky and Masny, 2013:1) (my interpretation of curriculum tactics and applications). Like Inna Semetsky and Diana Masny in their book *Deleuze and Education*, I also find these as 'three interconnected problematic fields' (2013:1), because they are not ontologically emancipatory, and they do not systematically and wholly address what Ted T. Aoki defines as the praxis in between (planned and lived) curriculum (Aoki, 2005). Semetsky and Masny characteristically say that education has to be understood also by reference to Gilles Deleuze as 'explicated by experience and culture' (Semetsky and Masny, 2013:1) and the praxis of such we should call pedagogy in the context of this book. Michalinos Zembylas who we will refer to in Part 3 (Synapsis II) of this book with regards to the notions of desire and affect, notes that in fact pedagogy can manifest in the condition of formal learning (what we can call the site of pedagogy (Di Leo, Jacobs, and Lee, 2002), and curation of a learning environment) but does not signify such. Instead, pedagogy can be seen as the 'relational encounter among individuals through which many possibilities for growth are created' (Zembylas, 2007:332). The praxis of such we will refer to as currere, which we will approach as perlocutionary act that opens up to the possibility for liberation and growth but is firmly rooted in critical thinking and contemplation – praxis in reality.

Like reality (Haraway, 2003:6), we can regard praxis as active verb, as an event. Jason Wallin in his essay 'Morphologies for a Pedagogical Life' notes the endo-systemic maladies of education and the currere, noting that falsely we (as of educators) have been accustomed to thinking of the curriculum as a noun' (Wallin, 2013a:205). Instead, currere – the praxis of pedagogy – is a verb, and if seen as a definitive noun and ascribed a reality it becomes inert, and therefore not just incapable to lead to change but also harmful (Whitehead, 1929:1–2). Currere theory was pioneered by William Pinar presented at the 1975 Annual Meeting of the American Research Association (Pinar, 2004) and highlighted the autobiographical character of pedagogy from the point of view of the educator as pilgrim towards their own initiation. In practice, currere is referred upon as a practical exercise of self-reflection and writing, quite standardised for teachers in training and pedagogists, quite unknown to educators who teach their own specialist subject as part of their academic practice and who are normally subject to their own domain's intricacies. Wallin attempts a reterritorialisation of the concept of currere looking at the latter from a Deleuze and Guattari perspective offering an 'onto-ecology or counter-cartography' (Wallin, 2013b:35) of pedagogy and refocusing on collective mentorship against 'institutionalised myopia' (Wallin, 2013b:49), which we will discuss more extensively in Part 3 (Synapsis II) of this book. For now, it is important to address in response that to currere demands a collegium (McNay, 1995:106) – 'a virtual ecology of qualitative multiplicity for extension and reference' (Wallin, 2013b:49). In the context of this book, to currere is a praxis beyond discipline, the self-reflective and disclosive praxis of pedagogy that promotes erudition. It is situated in between the curriculum and the lived experience of learning. It lingers and contemplates and regards all counterparts of the pedagogical act: teachers, learners, and the environment which the learning takes place within.

Notes

1 my emphasis
2 Paraphrasing architect and theorist Aristedes Antonas in his book *The Pulp of Things* (Ο Πολτός των Πραγμάτων) who says, 'humanity and reality are the same malady' (2020:55).
3 An earlier version of this section first appeared in the paper 'Pediagogy of Practice: Creating Pivotal Cultures for Learning Architecture' co-authored with Benjamin Powell in *Teaching-Learning-Research: Design and Environments Architecture* AMPS Proceedings Series 22.1 Manchester School of Architecture; AMPS Manchester: 02–04 December 2020.

References

Alexandre, L. and Besnier, J. M. (2018) *Do Robots Make Love? From AI to Immortality*. London: Octopus Books.

Aoki, Ted T. (2005) *Curriculum in a New Key: The Collected Works of Ted T. Aoki*. Ed by W. F. Pinar and R L. Irwin. Mahwah, NJ: Lawrence Erlbaum.

Burnet, J. (1968) *Aristotle on Education: Extracts from Ethics and Politics*. Cambridge: Cambridge University Press.

Camus, A. (1948) *The Plague*. New York: Alfred Knopf.

Cole, D. R. (2013) 'Affective Literacies: Deleuze, Discipline, and Power' in I. Semetsky and D. Masny (eds.), *Deleuze and Education*. Edinburgh: Edinburgh University Press. 94–111.

Cole, D. R. (2021) *Education, the Anthropocene and Deleuze/Guattari*. Leiden and Boston: Brill.

Collins, P. M. (1990) 'Aristotle and the Philosophy of Intellectual Education' in *The Irish Journal of Education/Iris Eireannach an Oideachais*, Vol. 24 (2), 62–88.

Deleuze, G. (1994) *Difference and Repetition*. Trans by Paul Patton. London: Continuum.

Dewey, J. (1931) *Art as Experience*. New York: Milton, Blach and Co.

Di Leo, J. R., Jacobs, W. and Lee, A. (2002) 'The Sites of Pedagogy' in *Symplokē*, Vol. 10 (1/2), 7–12.

Fisher, M. (2009) *Capitalism Realism; Is There No Alternative?* Winchester: Zero Books.

Freire, P. (2017) [1970] *Pedagogy of the Oppressed*. Trans by Myra Bergman Ramos. London: Penguin.

Freire, P. (2021) *Pedagogy of Hope, Reliving Pedagogy of the Oppressed*. London: Bloomsbury.

Glasser, W. (1998) *Choice Theory: A New Psychology of Personal Freedom*. New York: Harper Perennial.

Giroux, H. A. (2020) *On Critical Pedagogy*. 2nd ed. London: Bloomsbury.

Greene, M. and Macrine, S. L. (2009) 'Teaching as Possibility: A Light in Dark Times' in S. L. Macrine (ed.), *Critical Pedagogy in Uncertain Times: Hopes and Possibilities*. Cham: Palgrave Macmillan. 81–94.

Han, B.-C. (2015) *The Burnout Society*. Stanford, CA: The University of Stanford Press.

Han, B.-C. (2017) *The Scent of Time*. Trans by Daniel Steuer. Cambridge: Polity.

Haraway, D. (2003) *A Companion Species Manifesto: Dogs, People and Significant Otherness*. Chicago: Prickly Paradigm Press.

Hooks, B. (2003) *Teaching Community: A Pedagogy of Hope*. New York and London: Routledge.

Mayo, P. (2020) 'Critical Pedagogy in Difficult Times' in S. L. Macrine (ed.), *Critical Pedagogy in Uncertain Times: Hopes and Possibilities*. Cham: Palgrave Macmillan. 33–43.

McFarlane, B. (2005) 'The Disengaged Academic' in *Higher Education Quarterly*, Vol. 59 (4), 296–312.

McNay, I. (1995) 'From the Collegial Academy to the Corporate Enterprise: The Changing Cultures of Universities' in T. Schuller (ed.), *The Changing University?* Milton Keynes: Open University Press. 105–115.

Morton, T. (2018) *Being Ecological*. London: Pelican.

Pessoa, F. (2010) *The Book of Disquiet*. Trans by Margaret Jull Costa. London: Serpent's Tail.

Pinar, W. (2004) *What is Curriculum Theory?* London: Routledge.

Powell, B. and Psarologaki, L. (2020) 'Pediagogy of Practice: Creating Pivotal Cultures for Learning Architecture' in L. Sanderson and S. Stone (eds.), *AMPS Proceedings Series 22.1. Teaching – Learning – Research*. Manchester: Manchester School of Architecture. December 2–4, 2020. 310–318.

Preciado, P. B. (2019) *An Apartment on Uranus*. London: Fitzcarraldo.

Psarologaki, L. (2020) 'Making Architects in Agile Studios: A Manifesto for Situated Architectural Education' in *The Cambridge Architecture Journal Scroope 29*. Cambridge: The University of Cambridge. 16–31.

Rabinbach, A. (1992) *The Human Motor: Energy, Fatigue, and the Origins of Modernity*. Berkeley and Los Angeles: University of California Press.

Robb, F. C. (1943) 'Aristotle and Education' in *Peabody Journal of Education*, Vol. 20 (4), 202–213.

Semetsky, I. (2013) 'Learning with Bodymind: Constructing the Cartographies of the Unthought' in D. Masny (ed.), *Cartographies of Becoming in Education: A Deleuze-Guattari Perspective*. Rotterdam: Sense. 71–91.

Semetsky, I. and Masny, D. (2013) 'Introduction: Unfolding Deleuze' in *Deleuze and Education*. Edinburgh: Edinburgh University Press.

Tachibana, K. (2012) 'How Aristotle's Theory of Education Has Been Studied in Our Century' in *Studia Classica*, Vol. 3, 21–67.

Wallin, J. (2013a) 'Morphologies for a Pedagogical Life' in I. Semetsky and D. Masny (eds.), *Deleuze and Education. Deleuze Connections*. Edinburgh: Edinburgh University Press. 196–214.

Wallin, J. (2013b) 'Get Out from Behind the Lectern' in D. Masny (ed.), *Cartographies of Becoming in Education: A Deleuze-Guattari Perspective*. Rotterdam: Sense. 35–52.

Whitehead, A. N. (1929) *The Aims of Education and Other Essays*. New York: The Free Press.

Zembylas, M. (2007) 'Risks and Pleasures: A Deleuzeoguattarian Pedagogy of Desire' in *Education in British Educational Research Journal*, Vol. 33 (3), 331–347.

Part 3

Synapsis II

Deligny and Deleuze; Post-Humanist Desires

curriculum builders, beware sick buildings
shrill claims to know what teaching is
reduced to doing

(Koops, 2014:34)

This Part (Synapsis II) continues the philosophical discussion on erudition and its clinical cartography in the context of contemporary advanced capitalist societies. It focuses on posthumanism highlighting the urgent need to address the idiosyncratic characteristics of contemporary pedagogy and the need to address the humanity in pedagogy more broadly. This chapter critically defines the concepts of 'desire' and 'wanting' as constitutional terms of a pedagogy and erudition. It presents the latter (in the context of education) as a construct that is stronger and more pertinent today with regards to learning and living in comparison to what we understand as society. The chapter introduces Synapsis III (next Part) with the definition of the learners' network as a people-in-becoming having individual and collective desires and which presents illnesses. The latter create topologies and common neuronal pathologies, such as anxiety disorders explained in Part 1 and 2. This Part will also establish the concept of utopian currere, based on Darren Webb's concept of utopian educator and situates pedagogy among the learning components. Synapsis I (Part 2) of this book, established the term erudition as the lost/missing culture in contemporary education and pedagogy and discussed the latter within the context of –the absence of – contemplative praxis, a post-Aristotelian schole. It is important to add to the definition of pedagogy that the contemplative praxis referred to in Synapsis I is not the commonly misinterpreted theoria of Aristotle, which is also emphatically an activity (Burnet, 1903:8), an event of learning via living and acting by critically reflecting and thinking. Contemplation is presented here as non-passive immersion and therefore constitutive act of learning,

DOI: 10.4324/9781003220619-4

with the latter being ontologically associated with pedagogy. In this context we can define the verb currere as to contemplate and exercise an educational human-to-human experience (Lewko, 2014:168) of erudition, which can be effectively post-human, because it ontologically carries an ecological and political dimension of pedagogy.

The political dimension of erudition (as with education and pedagogy) and therefore of currere and learning, is deeply rooted in machinic and eco-systemic phenomena and events. These are systems and infrastructures of education specifically, but also statutory and regulatory machines and networks of operation, and national and international frameworks of economic and social nature. One of these is a phenomenon that has been identified in the environmental sciences and is introduced here because as discussed previously pedagogy is ontologically linked to ecological scopes, as well as the individual and the state and has – or ought to acquire – a post-humanist dimension. This phenomenon is the 'shifting baseline syndrome' or SBS defined by marine biologist Daniel Pauly in an essay about the environmental parameters of fisheries (Pauly, 1995). Masashi Soga and Kevin J. Gaston explore Pauly's concept in terms of implications in and potential responses from the wider environment (Soga and Gaston, 2018:222–230). Its definition (human-centred) as pathology in the societal and scientific views and actions that may shape the future in one or another way is fundamentally pedagogical, is one of post-human erudition, of a nature-culture continuum (Massumi, 2002:11). Shifting baseline syndrome according to Soga and Gaston refers to the observation of a systemic and gradual change in terms of the extent of what is accepted as standard or normative because of lack of historical data and/or experience of past conditions. It implies a gradual difference in what people expect and what is desirable and the 'establishment and use of inappropriate baselines' (Soga and Gaston, 2018:222). One can argue that this is in principle observed in the professional sector of higher education and in the wider perceptions about education as well as in environmental science and the natural environment more broadly, particularly in the UK but also Europe more intensively in the last fifteen years.

The learning itself and its constitutive elements suffer from a notable and continuous 'move of the goalposts' in all areas. This is observed more clearly and as systemic phenomenon in countries where Higher Education is not regarded less of a commons, and more of a service to be consumed and where issues of accessibility and access to opportunity are picked up and addressed by institutions. The latter has even more so stretched the extent to which SBS is observed and of course widens the scope of impact of learning. In vocation and practice-led curricula, which we will discuss in Parts 4 and 5, this is even more so intensified. There is a critical chiasm between what is called the professional sector – and which sets the expectations for the profile of a graduate, under SBS – and the academy with the latter generally seen as the one not in line. As highlighted previously, quoting Giroux, pedagogy is never innocent, but it is important to assign responsibility where it really lies and that is in its own merit a critical and contemplative praxis rooted in sociocultural practices and contexts, education is inherently a part of, as well as the real-world experiences and life itself.

Post-Humanist Citizenship

There are pedagogical implications around the phenomenon of the SBS, and which we can associate to the collegium and issues of citizenship in learning, pedagogy, erudition, and the praxis of currere as we defined it in the previous Part. Citizenship in education is neither a novel concept nor an emerging practice in pedagogy. On the contrary it has been a constitutive part of education and pedagogy since Plato's Academy, then associated with democracy and politics (and therefore one's moral obligation to the place of residency), virtue (goodness) and of course culture and the cultivation of character (ethics) within a community, which we can also detect in the work of Aristotle. As Burnet highlights particularly for the ancient Greeks the atom of community (and therefore education) was the family. Although Plato implies its dissolution altogether Aristotle focused more on the risks of such rather than its positive impact on cultivating an ecology (Burnet, 1903:132). This is perhaps because the Athenian family was not the nuclear unit that we have been idolising for so long together with romanticising the first democracy, where women and slaves constituted most of the citizenship but had no visible political rights, certainly none compared to today's modern societies. On the other hand, as Burnet also notes, there is the French tradition and long-standing treatise of family as direct pedagogical opposition to what the state represents (Burnet, 1903:133). Although this book does not address pedagogy and education from the point of view of cognition and the psychology of the individual who is learning – this was another long tradition recent literature on pedagogical practice has transcended – attachment theory suggests that from an ecological perspective, the impact of the nucleus of the family and secure attachment may reflect on and relate to the maladies of reflexive impotence (Fisher, 2009) and deferral we discussed in Parts 1 and 2. This is because 'secure individuals [and therefore communities (collegia) and networks of such] are optimistic about coping with stress, likely to relate better to others, have greater capacity for concentration and cooperation and are more confident and resilient' (Fleming, 2008:39); they are therefore more prone to meaningful and ethical studentship and citizenship.

In the contemporary world of University education state related curricula are coloured with a 'fixation on technique, the economy and vocalisation' (Welton, 1995 quoted in Fleming, 2008:33). This is brought forward by the forces of neoliberalism, and the academic study of subjects that are fundamentally vocational (i.e., rooted in apprenticeship, a techne, and/or professionally accredited through prescription/ PSRB processes) is becoming a stiff body of planned curriculum overtaking lived curriculum and currere (in between). There lies a point of stress and power, which lies within the domain of critical pedagogy and currere desire, and manifests in educational citizenship. Citizenship in education, is defined here drawing from the thought of Pocock (1995:30) and Habermas (2000) brought up by Clarence W. Joldersma and Ruth Deakin Crick in the essay 'Citizenship, Discourse Ethics and an Emancipatory Model of Lifelong Learning'. More towards the political model of praxis in a community (a collegium) and beyond the affective recognition of an ethics of discourse against violence (Joldersma and Deakin Crick, 2009:137), a pedagogy of educational citizenship is emancipatory and experiential; it is Pessoa's erudition of sensibility (Pessoa, 2010:77) that presumes 'lifelong learning, a vital aspect of the continuing active role citizens might assume in society' (Joldersma and Deakin Crick, 2009:137). This however is less a state of harmony thinkers present and more a crisis and disquiet, where the learner and educator are both part of the state machine and potentially challenging it, engaging therefore in praxis of 'explicit critique and active legitimisation' (Joldersma and Deakin Crick, 2009:140) – a praxis of democracy by experiencing the lifeworld of learning.

A pedagogy of democracy (and not necessarily a democratised curriculum per se) can be much more than a platform for empowering a learner's becoming a member for a participatory community mode of living and practicing discourse ethics (Joldersma and Deakin Crick, 2009:149); it can offer a pragmatic and replicable experience of emancipatory erudition that considers a nature-culture continuum (Massumi, 2002:11). Such would be post-anthropocentric not because it will focus less on the human individuals who can be seen as components of the educational and pedagogical praxis (namely learners and educators) and more on the enhancement of the non-human elements (tools). It would be post-anthropocentric because it will focus on the social praxis of pedagogy among and in-between the learning components and will regard those as cyborg citizens, not separate and autonomous somatic entities (Ceder, 2020:87). John Dewey in his seminal book *Democracy and Education* reflects on Aristotelian thought on civic life (bios politikos) to draw the line between menial and liberal education and to exalt the latter as related with schole (2018:270). He notes though that to understand democracy in and of education as directly and de facto linked to civic life and community or society implies the formation of associations that can be both good and bad and to accept such with a view that citizenship (end therefore democracy in education) means 'free and equitable intercourse which springs from a variety of shared interests makes intellectual stimulation unbalanced. Diversity of stimulation means novelty, and novelty means challenge to thought' (Dewey, 2018:91).

In-Between Democracy

A democratic pedagogy is different to a democratic or democratised education, or of a democratic schooling. Naoshi Kira (2004) notes that

> [d]emocratic education has larger meanings than democratic schooling, as reflected, for example, in the fact that democratization of education has at least the following three meanings: 'universalization of educational opportunities;' 'decentralization of education systems;' and 'participatory practices in school and class.'

A democratic pedagogy is a collective praxis based on diversity, equity, and equality. It can be assigned (new) dimensions, directions and meaning in contemporary and future educational settings. 'Being able to explicitly engage with the stories, values, attitudes and resources which constitute the students' lifeworld . . . is a powerful educational foundation which is crucial for the formation of the learning power necessary for what we are calling an emancipatory model of lifelong learning (Joldersma and Deakin Crick, 2009:143). This is a democracy of learning, and an education of 'relationatility', what Simon Ceder defines as 'edu-activity' (Ceder, 2020:86–87). Ceder draws from post-human approaches such as the seminal work of Rosi Braidotti (in terms of the posthuman) and Karen Barad (in terms of relationality) to locate education between its two ontological, topological and constitutional components (educators and the ones to be educated) and notes that it takes place (as an event of becoming) in a 'gap that is neither placed at the student's side nor on the teacher's side' and that most importantly '[t]he distinct subjects are needed for the idea of the gap to work' (Ceder, 2020:87). This makes education (and therefore the pedagogical praxis) an 'intersubjective subject' where the gap facilitating the learning is a social domain within which the non-human aspects are not reduced to (passive) tools that facilitate the learning (Ceder, 2020:95). A creative democracy in pedagogy, as defined by Pignatelli (1999) and Dewey (1991), is potentially reached through addressing issues of intersubjective desires. We can imbue desire in pedagogies situated and dwelled in-between, to allow for a better future by means of culture. We can employ deferral, disquiet and schole by

introducing nascent modes of 'switching on, logging in, booting up, surf-
ing, processing' (Cole, 2014:16) in affective ways to enable the need for
cultivating erudition through contemplative praxis. In such way, we can
employ the so seen as maladies of capitalism realism (Fisher, 2009) towards
transformative change, starting from 'original entanglement of everything
and the idea that knowledge consists of temporary and situated realities of a
multidimensional constantly changing world' (Ceder, 2020:104). In the latter, learner, educator, and world cannot be separate (Ceder, 2020:105). In a
contemporary world where changing is the norm, when 'education narrows
down its scope . . . it reduces a culture's power to adapt to change' (Bruner,
1996:15) and therefore its ontological capacity to foster erudition (of any
kind in Pessoa's triplet).

The positioning of desire – beyond its libidinal force of pleasure – in
terms of will and praxis in education gives some insightful streams of
thought particularly when examined against contemporary and past illness
associated with learning modes, experiences, and patterns. Although Aristotle in his Ethics implies that desire leads to praxes of the (morally) weak
(and therefore is more humane), he does not directly and exclusively link its
operative condition of difference (will) with a so-called intellectual process.
In Aristotelian thought, will is seen as a process of acting out of power – a
practicable – whilst desire is seen as a process acting out of passion – a
thinkable – (Burnet, 1903:73). The question is what happens when will
and desire collide, given that when different desires do this leads to idleness. The will has to be educated itself to endure the strains of civilisation
and desire is a primitive form of affective drive for life. Anson Rabinbach,
exploring the neurasthenia brought to learners from modern life, notes that
when power of desire is negative, will is weak, and the need for education
is suppressed creating an 'inferior student whose impaired performance [is]
a consequence of the exhaustion' (Rabinbach, 1992:152) but is not seen
as endemic or inherent to the realities of learning. On the contrary it tends
to become individualised and generalised[1] at the same time. Interestingly,
critical theorist of pedagogy and founder of the concept of critical pedagogy
Henry Giroux, in his book *On Critical Pedagogy* (2020), notes that transformative pedagogy is rooted in democracy (Giroux, 2020:85) and associates progressive education with desire. He says '[p]edagogy presupposes
that [learners and educators] are moved by their passions and motivated, in
part, by affective investments they bring to the learning process' (Giroux,
2020:94) and it has the potential to become transformative when it takes
place in-between, neither purely theorised (Aoki's planned curriculum), nor
de factor commodified (Aoki's lived curriculum within a capitalised education) (Giroux, 2020:91) – the praxis of active citizenship, and erudition of
sensibility.

Desire Networks[2]

Deleuze and Guattari say that '[i]f desire produces, its product is real. If desire is productive, it can be productive only in the real world and can produce only reality' (1983:26). To address the malady of humanity and reality effectively by education and ensure we consider the complexities previously addressed we must go beyond singular theories of education of desire. We need to question the constitutive structures of institutions and communities in situated learning looking at non-typical and human-centred ecologies and pedagogies of being – networks. To explore the notion of network as the constitutive structure of a community (what we will define in the next Part as a learners' people-in-becoming) we can draw from enigmatic and visionary pedagogue Fernand Deligny, who remained for a long time a mystified and marginalised (or more accurately missed from most pedagogical treatise) figure of pedagogy perhaps because he was an 'amateur' and consistently opposed the structure of institutions of any kind, criticising the doctrines of his time (Hilton, 2015). Deligny, who became Deleuze and Guattari's inspiration on the rhizome, invested his life work on studying the aberrant topologies and autistic children's learning in France starting in the 50's. His poetic writing in the late published *The Arachnean and Other Texts* (2015) highlighted the weaving of a network as a (better future) mode of being that is different to society because it allows multitudes of species and methods and allows survival in times of crisis, noting that a network can disappear or become an institution, yet it can be characterised by both collective and individual will, desire and agency. It is a situated 'enduring phenomenon, a vital necessity' (Deligny, 2015:47). In line with Pessoa's erudition of sensibility, Deligny criticises '[t]he human-that-we-are [which] is the product of a long process of domestication' (Deligny, 2015:76). Wanting (desire), Deligny says, is an epiphenomenon of such construct. We will approach it here as an ontological dynamic condition aiming for transformative change, a shift brought to an education that is not there to accommodate or 'strengthen the status and . . . keep in place much of the frequently perceived ills, economic, social, and environmental' (Mayo, 2020:35). If we're not engaging in a 'wanting-to-make' (Deligny, 2015:50) the will for change disappears, so does the opportunity for praxis. Deligny's network is Ceder's post-human learning (Ceder, 2019:103), is Barad's inter-relationality of a world that 'articulates itself differently' (Barad, 2007:149). Deligny's reality of a network is a post-human inter-relational reality. He asks 'what if beings do not distinguish themselves from this external reality? Each time the table, bowl, and chair are encountered anew, it amounts to a rediscovery . . . a being who is unaware of being and of being apart, distinct from the bowl, chair, and table, lacks this assurance' (Deligny, 2015:62–63). For Deleuze and

Guattari, desire is lack and we must 'untie the pseudo-bond between desire and pleasure as an extrinsic measure' (Deleuze and Guattari, 1987:150) and understand desire in its own potential for an achieved state to fill itself as lack, and allow beings to find themselves (within a network) (Deleuze and Guattari, 1987:156). It in 'itself results from a highly developed, engineered setup rich in interactions' (Deleuze and Guattari, 1987:215).

Deligny also links the network (and its constitutive self as desiring machine) with responsibility (Deligny, 2015:53) (and therefore citizenship). Responsibility – as discussed in previous Parts – is fundamental to education and (critical) pedagogy, and its situation among (a people, environments, and things) rather than the atomised learner (Mayo, 2020:39) in the network. This is not a negation of identity; on the contrary it has to do with the becoming that stems from 'connectedness and . . . the notion of participant membership [that] has to feed into our conceptions of democratic citizenship' (Greene and Macrine, 2020:88) and allows access to 'the radical self' (Zembylas, 2007:332). If we see the latter as resistance (to the existing, the status quo and its ill affordances) we can agree with Michalynos Zembylas that the risks associated to desire constitute the potentiality to resist (Zembylas, 2007:337) and that 'teaching and learning are acts of desire' (Zembylas, 2007:333), drawing from Todd (1998) and Kelly (1997). A pedagogy of desire within a network can indeed become transformative praxis – an erudition, a critical contemplative act that calls the relata of education (the educator and the one to be educated) to 'be more, to render themselves complex' (Pignatelli, 1999:340). Desire and network are associated by Deleuze and Guattari, and Zembylas, through Deligny's *The Arachnean*. Zembylas notes that a Deleuzo-guattarian desire is an assemblage of heterogenous elements (and therefore post-human), it is an event 'defined by zones of intensity, multiplicity and flux' (Zembylas, 2007:337). Deligny on the other hand differentiates the event of a network to society because the latter does not allow for diversity of species and therefore is seen as a constraining and exclusive construct. He says that 'this thing we call society in which beings conscious of being enjoy themselves to the fullest can become so restrictive, so bent on subjugation, that networks are woven outside the grip of the abusive society' (Deligny, 2015:41). We can extract a fundamentally pedagogical ecology from these associations, one that allows for aberrant constructs among the relata of the educational act and can project towards future possibilities embracing the flux and change of the contemporary reality pedagogy ought to be prescribed within but not limiting itself by its own norms.

Utopian Currere

We must once again stress at this point the importance of pedagogy as critical praxis that is situated in between the relata of learning – a network of desires where the latter is neither Freud's libidinal drive, nor Lacan's lack (Zembylas, 2007:335). Desires manifest in critical pedagogy as culture, as defined by Bruner: 'a complex symbolic apparatus of myths, statutes, precedents, ways of talking and thinking' (Bruner, 1996:29). This creates an event of non-exclusive allegiance of belonging (Bruner, 1996:30) through collective conception of what is not necessarily predictable but imagines as possible (Greene and Macrine, 2020:82). The notion of imagination in erudition leads us to a fundamental concept of critical and democratic pedagogist: the utopian educator, coined by Darren Webb reading on Freire. Driven by desire, Webb argues, we can develop a pedagogy of kinship, communication, intimacy, and curiosity – actual and virtual. In such a critical and progressive pedagogical model there is a culture of citizenship and desire; a collective 'we' and the distance between what is lived (experience) and what is learnt (knowledge) is diminishing. Only then, he says, we can use our intellectual and cultural weapons to challenge the existing institutional liberalism (Powell and Psarologaki, 2020:311). Webb asks for pedagogy of longing, hope, liberation, imagination, and the cultivation of the possibility of learners to organise life in new ways, which can lead to better ways of being (Webb, 2020b) and prevent a systemic dystopia. Webb presents two concepts of educational utopia based on critical and progressive pedagogies, from we which we can extract most prominently the notion of utopia-as-process, which is among others

> an open-ended process of becoming rather than a static representation of a single state of affairs . . . a process of exploring new possibilities, [and] unmasking the operation of power so that new open, partial, fluid, spaces of possibility can emerge.
>
> (Webb, 2013:280–281)

Webb's desire may still be firmly rooted in the human condition (Webb, 2020a) but it is not limited to being for the human per se, because it implies networks and affiliation (collegia) outside the institutional. It can be seen as linked to Deligny's notion of network, and Barad's inter-relationality, therefore acquiring post-human characteristics although not de droid post-anthropocentric.

To discuss utopian currere in the context of a post-human network and erudition as culture and sensibility, we must draw once again from Henry Giroux and his articulation of critical pedagogy. Effective education lives in jeopardy says Bruner (Bruner, 1996:15) and we should not per se attempt a politicisation of education through critical pedagogy. We must however seek to accept and address its being political (evoking citizenship) not necessarily by protest (activism is not contemplative) but by praxis of in between currere, which is transformative, diverse, intimate, and emancipatory act of contemplative reflection encompassing practice (Mezirow, 1995:10). A utopian currere is based in critical pedagogies that seek to educate hopes (Webb, 2013:284). To currere critically means to practice a utopian pedagogy, which is situated at the risky 'gap' among the relata, in the desires and inter-relationalities, afforded by the contemporary ever-changing world. To do so – accepting that we are not currently up to the task, as Webb notes (Webb, 2013:286) – we must rethink our ontological vocabularies and words that frame education and pedagogy, towards the learning of and for a people-in-becoming, the post-anthropocentric nature-culture continuum (Massumi, 2002:11), and new, more diverse meanings in culture, citizenship, and democracy.

Notes

1 A reference to GOD (generalised anxiety disorder), notably hitting high-performing individuals.
2 An earlier version of this section first appeared in the paper "Pediagogy of Practice: Creating Pivotal Cultures for Learning Architecture" co-authored with Benjamin Powell in *Teaching-Learning-Research: Design and Environments Architecture* AMPS Proceedings Series 22.1 Manchester School of Architecture; AMPS Manchester: 02–04 December 2020.

References

Barad, K. (2007) *Meeting the Universe Halfway: Quantum Physics and the entanglement of Matter and Meaning*. Durham: Duke University Press.
Bruner, J. (1996) *The Culture of Education*. Cambridge, MA and London: Harvard University Press.
Burnet, J. (ed.) (1903) *Aristotle on Education. Extracts from the Ethics and Politics*. Cambridge: Cambridge University Press.
Ceder, S. (2019) *Towards a Posthuman Theory of Educational Relationality*. London and New York: Routledge.
Cole, D. R. (2014) *Capitalised Education; An Immanent Materialistic Account of Kate Middleton*. Winchester: Zero Books.
Deleuze, G. and Guattari, F. (1983) *Anti-Oedipus*. Minneapolis and London: University of Minnesota Press.
Deleuze, G. and Guattari, F. (1987) *A Thousand Plateaus: Capitalism and Schizophrenia*. Trans by B. Massumi. Minneapolis and London: University of Minnesota Press.
Deligny, F. (2015) *The Arachnean and Other Texts*. Trans by Drew S. Burk and Catherine Porter. Minneapolis: Univocal Publishing.
Dewey, J. (1991) 'Creative Democracy – The Task Before Us' in J. A. Boydston (ed.), *John Dewey, The Later Works, 1925–1953, Vol. 14: 1939–1941*. Carbondale, IL: Southern Illinois University Press. 224–230.
Dewey, J. (2018) *Democracy and Education: An Introduction to the Philosophy of Education*. Gorham, ME: Myers Education Press.

Fisher, M. (2009) *Capitalism Realism: Is There No Alternative?* Winchester: Zero Books.

Fleming, T. (2008) 'A Secure Base for Adult Learning: Attachment Theory and Adult Education' in *The Adult Learner, The Journal of Adult and Community Education in Ireland,* Vol. 25, 33–53.

Giroux, H. (2020) *On Critical Pedagogy.* London: Bloomsbury.

Greene, M. and Macrine, S. L. (2020) 'Teaching as Possibility: A Light in Dark Times' in S. L. Macrine (ed.), *Critical Pedagogy in Uncertain Times: Hopes and Possibilities.* Cham: Palgrave Macmillan. 81–94.

Habermas, J. (2000) *The Inclusion of the Other: Studies in Political Theory.* Ed by C. P. Cronin and P. D. Greiff. Cambridge, MA: MIT Press.

Hilton, L. (2015) 'Mapping the Wander Lines: The Quiet Revelations of Fernand Deligny' *Los Angeles Review of Books*, July 2, 2015. https://lareviewofbooks.org/article/mapping-the-wander-lines-the-quiet-revelations-of-fernand-deligny.

Joldersma, C. W. and Deakin Crick, R. (2009) 'Citizenship, Discourse Ethics and an Emancipatory Model of Lifelong Learning' in M. Murphy and T. Fleming (eds.), *Habermas, Critical Theory and Education.* New York and London: Routledge. 137–152.

Kelly, U. A. (1997) *Schooling Desire: Literacy, Cultural Politics, and Pedagogy.* New York and London: Routledge.

Kira, N. (2004) 'Philosophy and Practice of Democratic Schooling: Education for the Development of Individuality and Responsibility' Discussion Paper No. 125. Graduate School of International Development, Nagoya University.

Kira, N. (2019) 'Dewey's Democratic Conception in Education and Democratic Schooling: Lessons from the United States for Japan in a Time of Democracy in Crisis' in *Educational Studies in Japan: International Yearbook*, Vol. 13, 55–66.

Koops, S. (2014) 'Calling Upstream/Dream' in W. Hurren and E. Hasebe-Ludt (eds.), *Contemplating Curriculum: Genealogies/Times/Places.* New York and Oxon: Routledge. 31–37.

Lewko, C. P. (2014) 'Lived Experiences of Loss: Living Perceptibly as a Teacher in New Familiarities' in W. Hurren and E. Sasebe-Ludt (eds.), *Contemplating Curriculum: Genealogies/Times/Places.* New York and London: Routledge.

Massumi, B. (2002) *Parables for the Virtual: Movement, Affect, Sensation.* Durham and London: Duke University Press.

Mayo, P. (2020) 'Critical Pedagogy in Difficult Times' in S. L. Macrine (ed.), *Critical Pedagogy in Uncertain Times: Hopes and Possibilities.* Cham: Palgrave Macmillan. 33–43.

Mezirow, J. (1995) 'Transformative Learning: Theory to Practice' in M. Walton (ed.), *Defence of the Lifeworld: Critical Perspectives on Adult Learning.* New York: SUNY Press.

Pauly, D. (1995) 'Anecdotes and the Shifting Baseline Syndrome of Fisheries' in *Trends in Ecology & Evolution*, Vol. 10 (10).

Pessoa, F. (2010) *The Book of Disquiet.* Trans by Margaret Jull Costa. London: Serpent's Tail.

Pignatelli, F. (1999) 'Education and the Subject of Desire' in *The Review of Education/Pedagogy/Cultural Studies*, Vol. 20 (4), 337–352.

Pocock, J. (1995) 'The Ideal of Citizenship Since Classical Times' in R. Beiner (ed.), *Theorizing Citizenship*. New York: SUNY Press. 29–52.

Powell, B. and Psarologaki, L. (2020) 'Pediagogy of Practice: Creating Pivotal Cultures for Learning Architecture' in L. Sanderson and S. Stone (eds.), *AMPS Proceedings Series 22.1. Teaching – Learning – Research*. Manchester: Manchester School of Architecture. December 2–4, 2020. 310–318.

Rabinbach, A. (1992) *The Human Motor: Energy, Fatigue, and the Origins of Modernity*. Berkeley and Los Angeles: University of California Press.

Soga, M. and K. J. Gaston (2018) 'Shifting Baseline Syndrome: Causes, Consequences, and Implications' in *Frontiers in Ecology and the Environment*, Vol. 16 (4), 222–230.

Todd, I. (1998) *Learning Desire: Perspectives on Pedagogy, Culture, and the Unsaid*. New York and London: Routledge.

Webb, D. (2013) 'Critical Pedagogy, Utopia and Political (Dis)Engagement' in *Power and Education*, Vol. 5 (3), 280–290.

Webb, D. (2020a) 'Paulo Freire and The Need for a Kind of Education in Hope' in *Cambridge Journal of Education*, Vol. 40 (4), 327–339.

Webb, D. (2020b) 'The Utopian Educator? Reflections on the Scope for Transformative Practice' in *Critical Pedagogies and Theories for Post-Compulsory and Informal Education*. Liverpool: Public talk, Centre for Educational Research (CERES) Liverpool John Moores University, October 28, 2020.

Zembylas, M. (2007) 'Risks and Pleasures: A Deleuzo-Guattarian Pedagogy of Desire in Education' in *British Educational Research Journal*, Vol. 33 (3), 331–347.

Part 4

Synapsis III

Maverick and Temperate;
A People-In-Becoming

'when knowledge is dead, they call it the academy'

(Preciado, 2019:50)

The previous parts of this book unfolded a network of pedagogical terms and ideas, starting with the relative ontologies of learning, education, pedagogy, and erudition, drawing from classic, traditional, and post-modernist thought. Erudition was defined using references to Fernando Pessoa's fragmented memoirs in *The Book of Disquiet* (Pessoa, 2010) with particular focus on notions of culture and sensibility, read in parallel with Paolo Freire's book *Pedagogy of the Oppressed* (2017) rendering critical education as liberating and transformative praxis, with social and political ramifications. This assemblage of literary and philosophical treatise was followed by a review of the role of curricula and currere in achieving erudition through notions of democracy, citizenship, and desire. This chapter unfolds the characteristics of the learners' network as a people. Two typologies of learning relata are identified: the maverick and the temperate. These are key actors in the learning network and are not binary or polarised. The maverick is capable of creatively and radically contributing to shaping the learning network. The temperate learner assigns satisfaction to learning and gains pleasure by being part of the network in line with very mentality of modern work life challenging the normative interpretation of Aristotelian ethics and politics in education (de Botton, 2010:106). It presents a critical analysis and reflection on learning that takes place under pedagogical frameworks accommodating vocalisation of education. This will allow for an insightful discussion around contemporary pedagogy and education as driven by institutional and ethnographical norms and will lead to a nomadic ethno-cartography of the learning body, which we will call relata (educators and the ones to be educated, both seen as learning entities).

DOI: 10.4324/9781003220619-5

The vocalisation of education is currently shaping the landscapes of pedagogy, in some respects with detrimental effect to the capacity of all learning relata to achieve erudition by means of culture and sensibility. Chad Wellmon reflects on sociologist Max Weber's work to note a pattern of exaggeration in terms of what The University can achieve. He says indicatively that

> The University has become, for many, a sacred institution, a keeper of devotional practices and self-sustaining forms of life. The sacralization of The University is, I'd suggest, not only naive but pernicious' and that at the same time and through long processes of systemic change the university as an intimate, intellectual community devoted to the scholarly life seemed to have faded.
>
> (Wellmon, 2017)

The most pertinent thing in Wellmon's article and Weber's lectures on politics and ethics is the interpretation of vocalisation as a monstrosity and loss of intellectuality, which created a dichotomy between one hand the university and the academy (scholarly collegium), and on the other hand the focus of such on knowledge and ethos within the learning, and which led to cultural anxieties, and in terms of the interpretation of Weber's work a sign of resignation (Wellmon, 2017). This is linked to the valorisation of education as part of a 'global culture of enterprise' (Cole, 2021:34) where meritocracy appears by means of analogy between education and henceforth acquired wealth and where 'the task at hand is to reconnect consciousness to everyday life through education' (Cole, 2021:70). At the same time, academic life (becoming collegium) acquires a culturally and ontologically autotelic ecology 'already foreclosed by a series of blinkers that construct disciplinary thought within highly coded territories of knowledge' (Wallin, 2013:43). This phenomenon is even more intensified in vocation-led curricula that are shaped by prescriptive standards and homogenised expectations of systems that may demand de droit the evolution of distinctive identity in curriculum-as-planned yet feed from on ad nauseam and concomitantly occurring policing and moving of the goalposts. The detriment becomes evident in the lived aspect of the curriculum, any radical attempt of currere and the culture of the educational relata as well as the pedagogy that takes place immanently, as an inter-relationality among them.

The maladies and stress related to contemporary vocational curricula relate to the maladies and stress of the capitalistic systems that support and define education and the very reasons specific vocational subjects are becoming sought after educational routes and institutionally profitable entities of both scholarship and professional training. The fact that they are vocational as well as academic subjects and must be delivered as such creates specific problematics that amplify issues of culture, citizenship and erudition in contemporary education and the chasm between what it represents to the world and what it practically accounts for. This relates back to the notes of Max Weber in the *Vocation Lectures* (2004) and the questions posed regarding the relationship and differences between a profession and scholarship (in a science) and interestingly sees the latter as encompassing desire and a future (Weber, 2004:11). He sees beyond the discipline-specific progress scholarship which he regards as a fraction in the scope of education (Weber, 2004:12) and associates the continuous pursue of progress with the phenomenon of tedium (Weber, 2004:13). The latter was defined in Part 2 (Synapsis I) as a malady from loss of contemplative praxis, which we defined as post-Aristotelian schole. A scholar therefore becomes an educational relata that can learn and educate, it is a cyborg teacher-student entity that contributes to a culture. This affective dynamism the scholar (the entity who practices currere and schole) encompasses can be potentially muted and mutated by the confines of vocational agendas of greater magnitude that the curriculum or subject and are beyond institutional remit but regard the social and economic status of the profession under representation.

The Vocation of Becoming Anthropos[1]

One of the concepts Max Weber discusses in the context of education in the essay 'Science as a Vocation' is inconvenience. He notes that 'the first task of any competent teacher is to teach . . . students to acknowledge inconvenient facts' (Weber, 2004:22). While this refers to firm pedagogical approaches it is also deeply rooted in humanism in pedagogy. To transcend this towards a post-humanist erudition that is a produce of ecological praxis, we must understand the oxymoron of vocational curricula that are as well ontologically humanistic (not only human-centric but also for humans) and by contrast to classical thought based on learning by doing (practice/labour). The latter regard a real-life profession that is questionably brought in the learning (and currere) because as Weber says there is more to 'the tools of the trade' (Weber, 2004:24) when it comes to education, not the least because of the notable conflict of one's world views that ought to remain outside the learning environment, in the marketplace of life and may end up selling views in what ends up a warped democracy in classroom. On the contrary, this can become dynamic agency in currere when applied in the context of a pedagogy that aims in praxis to cultivate the individual relata (both educator and the one to be educated) through critical reflection, and this is utopian, post-anthropocentric pedagogy. It is the pedagogy Darren Webb calls for in the context of a radical education outside the Academy; an inhabitation of new morals, liberating imaginations, hopes, desires and possibilities, because the beauty of the latter is removed from The University (Webb, 2020). A pedagogy as such, Webb says, is one of intimacy that diminishes the distance between the assigned learning relata of teacher and learner and therefore is open to encompass an affective dimension. In such, scholars are systemically and individually capable of standing thinking in praxis beyond a landscape that is a 'state of simulation, a state in which we are obliged to replay all scenarios precisely because they have taken place already, whether actually or potentially' (Baudrillard, 1993:4) and therefore blind to open to new, unforeseen possibilities.

We may call a utopian post-anthropocentric pedagogy, a wild pedagogy. According to Geertz and Carstens, wilderness 'obliges us to embed new forms of being-presence and being-in-becoming on our pedagogical and research practices, seeking out new individual, social and environmental ecologies of production, action and expression' (Geertz and Carstens, 2021:II) and this means that we (as relata of, within and for learning) have to 'view ourselves in a constant and mutual state of responsibility for what happens in the . . . learning event as we affect and are being affected by everything else' (Lenz Taguchi, 2010:176). A schole then is a disclosure of Anthropos towards everything else where an individual (self) is rarely in one soma and one singular entity of a statutory, defined, and binary role, i.e., a student who is not educating others and therefore not a scholar, or an educator who is portrayed a leader (Weber, 2004:25) and therefore is reduced to a seller of knowledge to a silent market and at the same time the service on sale – a predefined product beyond evolution. Anthropos encompasses in its limited and vilified nature a disclosive post-human skill; the one that relates to the critical capacity of contemplative praxis, which is disclosive. In Plato's *Cratylus* and in Jacques Rancière's essay 'The Ignorant One's Lesson' (1991) we read Anthropos as the being who examines its observations and who knows its capacity of being contemplative and reflective (Rancière, 1991, 36). This may be the root of the dated and limited cogito ergo sum inverted, however we can read this beyond its references to cognition and consciousness of emancipation, which as Rancière notes, manifests as reflection and therefore is 'not about opposing manual knowledge . . . the intelligence of the tool and the worker, to the science of schools' (Rancière, 1991:36). Intellectual emancipation comes from contemplative praxis, from post-Aristotelian schole and from currere in critical, post-anthropocentric and utopian pedagogies that are disclosive and therefore open to new formations between the academy and the world it is situated within.

Ignorance and Disengagement

A pedagogy of hope and transformative change that leads to erudition of culture and sensibility is inconvenient because it being post-anthropocentric means it looks towards the future, yet it is not obsessed with being progressive per se. The future is a constitutive term of all critical pedagogies that can be disclosive because they are not dogmatic. Marc Augé reminds us that the future is an enterprise and manifests in social life subtend to others (Augé, 2014:2–3) and therefore post-anthropocentric. He also defines anthropologies (or any the study focused on, of and for Anthropos) as a 'coherent body of representation assembled over time and transmitted from generation to generation' (Augé, 2014:2) equating anthropology to culture. The latter has developed the toolkit for us to go beyond our 'native predisposition' (Bruner, 1996:15) and critical education embedded in culture must transmit this toolkit effectively. If it does not do so, it reduces the anthropological power to envisage and adapt to change which is the default mode of contemporary world (Bruner, 1996:15). This reduction is interpreted in a relative apathy of citizenship because the current state of affairs is rendered as 'impassable, immovable' (Augé, 2014:12). This is Mark Fisher's reflexive impotence (Fisher, 2009), and Byung-Chul Han's deferral (Han, 2017), an ideology of idle and non-contemplative nowness, which paralyses the thought about a future (Augé, 2014:3) which is a problem of politics and ethics, a problem of democracy and therefore a problem for erudition.

The loss of culture leads to a 'bare life (a thanato-technics) . . . [where] nothing promises duration or substance', 'profound boredom' (Han, 2015:18), a tedium, and the 'effects of a necropolitical technology of pleasure (Preciado, 2019:101). In such situation, education is expected to be defined by convenience, often masqueraded under the umbrellas of access and opportunity. On the contrary, it fails to be accessible and opportunistic because it loses its critically pedagogical basis, leading to ignorance and disengagement of the learning relata and therefore the learning itself. This is even more so prominent in vocationally prescribed curricula, where the contingencies that offer a getaway to radical and utopian pedagogies are dwarfed by the standardisation of curriculum-as-planned and concomitantly and ironically the bastardisation of the lived curriculum in relation to the in-between currere that carries the power to shape the culture of the critical, pedagogical praxis.

Pedagogical reflection is replaced by consultation and feedback and desire is replaced by will because it is convenient for the current state of affairs. Unfortunately, the latter is ill and because the attribute and substance of humanity lies towards distraction and absence and not haste or praxis (Rancière, 1991:55) (think for instance of the law of the least effort) we have acquired two concurrent and contradictory qualities; we have become autistic towards machinic achievement (obsessive with flesh-less, valorised progression and performance) and we developed low tolerance of boredom – a negative potency (Han, 2015:23). This is translated in asthenia manifesting in avoidance of labour (practicum) instead of a simplification of labour towards efficiency (an economy and ecology) (Rabinbach,

1992:176). Deferral, aboulia, ignorance, and disengagement are therefore symptomatic of the inherent maladies of the system itself they take place within in times of crisis and turbulence, and they are not caused by the crisis per se. Ignorance in particular is a broad systemic phenomenon in education both in the vilified bureaucratic machines of providing the service of The University and also the academic lived experience of learning and teaching, which hinders erudition and the capacity of pedagogy to become critical and therefore meaningfully progressive. Here comes another oxymoron; these are normally the ones to attempt a radical pedagogy and at the same the most submissive to prescriptive frameworks. Vocational curricula are often intensively infused with references, methods and tactics that target a 'profession' which equates falsely to 'practice'. The scholar then is tasked to become a reflective practitioner and currere becomes a contemplative, pedagogical praxis towards the 'creation and conduct of a reflective practicum' (Schön, 1987:156). Deeply rooted in the revived concept of the apprenticeship, vocational curricula and the scholar as practitioner-in-becoming have been evolving in the last two centuries in pedagogically intriguing ways and offer some insightful territory to explore broadly in the context of contemporary and future education and learning, not the least because these curricula live in the in-between space shaped by statutory rights and regulations (think of the 1997 Architects' Act)[2] and the policies and directions of HE Institutions, seemingly independent Schools and departments, and the plethora of academic leaders who become interchangeable nomads from School to School. Among those sit the educators (scholars themselves) – representing a role rather than individuals in capacity of praxis – as agents of culture and responsible for currere, who are themselves often disengaged and ignorant in the wider 'civic disengagement' (Macfarlane, 2005:296).

Maverick and Temperate[3]

Ignorance and disengagement are symptoms that are closely related to culture and cultural phenomena in contemporary times, including the loss and absence of culture in the wider expression of civic life as we came to know of it at least in the westernised and highly consumeristic world. As mentioned previously, these are approached here as symptoms, forming a symptomatologic perspective of educational and pedagogical thought. This approach is based on Gilles Deleuze's idea of a symptom creating new clinical entities and if attuned to desiring production can acquire an 'injunction to produce' (Tynan, 2010:153). The symptom that will allow a cartography of critical pedagogy of erudition is that of civic disengagement and impotence because the cultures that allowed citizenship to be part of vocational education are rooted out by the same forces that created civic disengagement (Marquand, 2004:2). The illness namely the pressures of the working practices and the alternate ways of leisure (Macfarlane, 2005:297) can facilitate schole as contemplative praxis and therefore give birth to the reflective practitioners, the scholars who do not only have a profession through which they learn and become emancipated but also a profession hey can shape and educate. As such, illness is viewed as a degree of health that implies life, which respectively implies practice that implies ways of living (Radman and Sohn, 2018:2,12n). In the extreme milieu of currere vocational education lies the Guattarian notion of psychosis, 'the therapeutic model for moving beyond the capitalistic assemblage . . . not just an illness, but the point at which all the models by which all the models by which subjectivity is produced and reproduced un daily life break down' (Tynan, 2010:159) and in which we can detect symptomatologically two quasi-subjective and inter-relational, pedagogical relata in the periphery of the learning topology: the maverick and the temperate.

The environment (learning world) in which the maverick and the temperate have been detected and are the flesh of, is the home of their illness and therapeutic, progressive opportunity for a new life – the studio or the lab. The studio, which represents not only the physical space for the practicum in vocational education, but also a platform of possibilities in its material and immaterial qualities where contingencies, dialogue and critique take place by reflective practice and by critical pedagogy, which encompasses a distinctive and situational condition of culture. This is approached here as the clinic – the site that can serve as site for observation, treatment of the ill, and education (Martin, 2018:188). The maverick and the temperate scholars are reflective practitioners in the making and engage in praxis that is characterised by vocational oppression as well as freedom of creativity and imagination that is academically translated as opportunity of commendable performance and avenue towards excellence. In this ontological paradox, they both remain in the periphery of the scholar body as non-normative paradigms of educational relata, and this is what makes them particularly significant with regards to critical and progressive pedagogies that encompass citizenship.

The maverick and the temperate act complementary and in double bind. The first term (the maverick) is borrowed from Owen Hopkins who sees the maverick as a practitioner who breaks the mould in a profession (Hopkins, 2016). The maverick scholar who can be a student, tutor, learner, coach, tutor, or mentor is a cyborg soma that responds to the civic disengagement and impotence by ignorance to the oppressive machines of prescriptive frameworks and the forces they impose. The maverick scholar who is not a genius (Hopkins, 2016:7) acts at the outskirts of the network, in the periphery of the prescribed learning and curriculum as planned. The maverick scholar shapes an aberrant practicum through schole that can be in jeopardy because they embrace the non-mainstream, the marginal connection to the syllabus and does not limit themselves to its interpretive capacity; on the contrary they engage with it by means of creative production. The maverick 'travel[s] freely the ladder of reflection, shifting' (Schön, 1987:164), as the learning weaves itself and develops into a coursework. The temperate scholar settles within a prescriptive practicum and the fulfilment of simplified labour stemming from the task of learning as practice, not necessarily exercising a performative preparation for educating others as part of lifelong learning and erudition by culture. The temperate scholar may also sit in the periphery of the examined learning relata in feedback studies and in consultation because they exercise a culture by silence, haunted by desire and the fixity of purpose (Pignatelli, 1998:338). The temperate and the maverick present the point of psychosis in the clinic of vocational education because the demonstrate its greatest weakness: 'the collective and individual responsibility to prepare for a practice and a life' (Cuff, 1991 quoted in Nicol and Pilling, 2000:7). This book and particularly this part will not examine how the maverick and the temperate may learn. As Gilles Deleuze notes, 'we do not know in advance how someone will learn' (Deleuze, 1994:165). On the contrary, we will examine them to create a symptomatologic cartography of the network of learning.

A People-in-Becoming

The maverick and the temperate are not de droid significant by quantitative presence in their learning environment however they become the relata the culture of critical pedagogy holds on to – the glue – and create the entourage for the network of a people-in-becoming in the pedagogical praxis of education that becomes erudition – schole. As Mark Bonta reminds us in his essay 'We're Tired of the Trees' Deleuze views future pedagogy as characterised by forces of control and instantaneity (Bonta, 2013:57). If we view these symptomatologically Instead of vilifying them, a network of a people-in-becoming (educational relata) can be weaved out of the geography they create. The forces of control evoke the profile of the temperate scholar and instantaneity (if not abused for the sake of continuum and deferral) evokes the maverick scholar. These are and have been immanent to the educating body, but may have however become progressively undetectable or fallen through the cracks because of the 'restrictive rules' demands and the scrutinised 'measure and report' approaches at Universities (Bonta, 2013:71). These are intensified by a robust skills-oriented training apparatus that invades assessment, which in itself becomes a system to be played, rigid enough to remain externally credible, readable and flexible enough to bend and accommodate (Bonta, 2013:71). In such, the maverick and temperate are hardly distinguished as of special idiosyncrasy or impact to pedagogical praxis, because the latter is not reviewed in order to sustain its imaginative and unpredictable face, on the contrary it goes under a gruesome health check (note the pun) to prove itself otherwise. In the case of creative (art and design related disciplines) and vocational (PSRB accredited) curricula, the dichotomy stretches the relata and currere to the point of educational psychosis (break point), which institutions and accrediting bodies (as well as the state, the Office for Students in the case of the UK, and TEF) must not only remain alert to, but address by ethical, political, and ecological action – by participation.

In the network of the pedagogy of learning, the relata form a people-to-become and a people-in-becoming that become constitutive to the culture the network represents and lives through. Critical for this is what Deligny describes as entour (around) and entourage (attendants or associates surrounding an individual) (Deligny, 2015:31). The around-ness and the relata that form the surrounding matter of such are the essence of the pedagogical substance that forms the network woven by and weaving the maverick and the temperate by desire and will respectively. Deligny also presents an interesting duet corresponding to our maverick and temperate – the ones wanting to and the ones having to, the fortuitous and the obligatory (Deligny, 2015:187). This is not a direct and exclusively made analogy, however there are threads of association and relativity. The fortuitous, which is associated to the maverick, is according to the Deligny the one that is engaged with the non-necessary as opposed to the obligatory (temperate) who has above all a bond of duty not for praxis but to complete the praxis (Deligny, 2015:191). As with being autistic according to Deligny, becoming fortuitous (maverick), obligatory (temperate) and/or and everything in between and beyond is not a matter of personification (Deligny, 2015:190), it is an ecological act and a matter of erudition by culture and by sensibility. There is a strong nomadological sense in Deligny's notion of the network and its capacity to be (mainly) post-anthropocentric (think of the WWW). It can be used pedagogically to 'advocate inclusive, connected, affective alliances to respond to systemic distortion and oppression' (Wilson and Kiely, 2002). Mapping (curriculum-as-planned) and rendering (lived curriculum) a network within the pedagogical praxis can help us (educators) 'retrieve our affective investments from reified categories and de-crystallize them to regain the power of becoming' (Roy, 2003:12); it can become a 'nomadic topos for true innovation' (Roy, 2003:69). It is nomadic because it resists the molecular and opens systemically to its irregularities, which are its constitutive qualities of becoming-a-network, and is composed by both identities and multiplicities, intensities and latitudes that are immanent and contract with its constitutive parts (the relata). The maverick and the temperate become the contractions that sustain the networks allowing them to become what they are not and with them contractions, create a complex and irregular topology of pedagogy that is inter-relational, situated, and peripheral. It depends on the experience of and in learning and not what the learning accounts for and it consciously denies being exhaustive, comprehensive, and dogmatic.

Notes

1 Paraphrasing Paolo Freire and the 'vocation of becoming more fully human' (Freire, 2017:40).
2 www.legislation.gov.uk/ukpga/1997/22/contents
3 The research-led learning and teaching case studies that led to this reflective account of the maverick and the temperate can be found in the paper 'Pediagogy of Practice: Creating Pivotal Cultures for Learning Architecture' co-authored with Benjamin Powell in *Teaching-Learning-Research: Design and Environments Architecture* AMPS Proceedings Series 22.1 Manchester School of Architecture; AMPS Manchester: 02–04 December 2020.

References

Augé, M. (2014) *The Future*. London: Verso.

Baudrillard, J. (1993) *The Transparency of Evil: Essays on Extreme Phenomena*. London: Verso.

Bonta, M. (2013) ' "We're Tired of Trees": Machinic University Geography Teaching After Deleuze' in I. Semetsky and D. Masny (eds.), *Deleuze and Education. Deleuze Connections*. Edinburgh: Edinburgh University Press. 57–73.

Bruner, J. (1996) *The Culture of Education*. Cambridge, MA and London: Harvard University Press.

Cole, D. R. (2021) *Education, the Anthropocene and Deleuze/Guattari*. Leiden and Boston: Brill.

Cuff, D. (1991) *Architecture: The Story of Practice*. Cambridge, MA: MIT Press.

de Botton, A. (2010) *The Pleasures and Sorrows of Work*. New York: Vintage.

Deleuze, G. (1994) *Difference and Repetition*. Trans by P. Patton. New York: Columbia University Press.

Deligny, F. (2015) *The Arachnean and Other Texts*. Trans by Drew S. Burk and Catherine Porter. Minneapolis: Univocal Publishing.

Fisher, M. (2009) *Capitalism Realism; Is There no Alternative?* Winchester: Zero Books.

Freire, P. (2017) [1970] *Pedagogy of the Oppressed*. Trans by Myra Bergman Ramos. London: Penguin.

Geertz, E. and Carstens, D. (2021) 'Pedagogies in the Wild' in *Matter: Journal of New Materialistic Research*, Vol. 2 (1), I–XIV.

Han, B.-C. (2015) *The Burnout Society*. Stanford, CA: University of Stanford Press.

Han, B.-C. (2017) *The Scent of Time*. Trans by Daniel Steuer. Cambridge: Polity.

Hopkins, O. (2016) *Mavericks: Breaking the Mould of British Architecture*. London: Royal Academy of Arts.

Lenz, Taguchi, H. (2010) *Going Beyond the Theory/Practice Divide in Early Childhood Education: Introducing an Intra-Active Pedagogy*. New York and London: Routledge.

Macfarlane, B. (2005) 'The Disengaged Academic' in *Higher Education Quarterly*, Vol. 56 (4), 296–312.

Marquand, D. (2004) *The Decline of the Public: The Hollowing-Out of Citizenship*. Cambridge: Polity.

Martin, K. (2018) 'Ecologies of Corporeal Space' in A. Radman and H. Sohn (eds.), *Critical and Clinical Cartographies: Architecture, Robotics, Medicine, and Philosophy. New Materialisms*. Edinburgh: Edinburgh University Press. 187–204.

Nicol, D. and Pilling, S. (2000) 'Architectural Education and the Profession: Preparing for the Future' in *Changing Architectural Education: Towards a New Professionalism*. London and New York: E&FN SPON Press.

Pessoa, F. (2010) *The Book of Disquiet*. Trans by Margaret Jull Costa. London: Serpent's Tail.

Pignatelli, F. (1998) 'Education and the Subject of Desire' in *Review of Education/Pedagogy/Cultural Studies*, Vol. 20, 337–352.

Powell, B. and Psarologaki, L. (2020) 'Pediagogy of Practice' in L. Sanderson and S. Stone (eds.), *AMPS Proceedings Series 22.1. Teaching – Learning – Research*. Manchester: Manchester School of Architecture. December 2–4, 2020. 310–318.

Preciado, P. B. (2019) *An Apartment on Uranus*. London: Fitzcarraldo.

Rabinbach, A. (1992) *The Human Motor: Energy, Fatigue, and the Origins of Modernity*. Berkeley and Los Angeles: University of California Press.

Radman, A. and Sohn, H. (2018) 'The Four Domains of the Plane of Consistency' in *Critical and Clinical Cartographies: Architecture, Robotics, Medicine, and Philosophy. New Materialisms*. Edinburgh: Edinburgh University Press. 1–20.

Rancière, J. (1991) *The Ignorant Schoolmaster: Five Lessons in Intellectual Emancipation*. Trans by K. Ross. Stanford, CA: Stanford University Press.

Roy, K. (2003) *Teachers in Nomadic Spaces. Deleuze and Curriculum*. New York: Peter Lang.

Schön, D. A. (1987) *Educating the Reflective Practitioner: Toward a New Design for Teaching and Learning in the Professions*. San Francisco: Josey-Bass Publishers.

Tynan, A. (2010) 'Deleuze and the Symptom: On the Practice and Paradox of Health' in *Deleuze Studies, Special Issue on Deleuze and the Symptom*, Vol. 4, No. 2. Edinburgh: Edinburgh University Press. 153–160.

Wallin, I. (2013) 'Get Out Behind the Lectern' in D. Masny (ed.), *Cartographies of Becoming in Education; A Deleuze-Guattari Perspective*. Rotterdam: Sense Publishers. 35–52.

Webb, D. (2020) 'The Utopian Educator? Reflections on the Scope for Transformative Practice' in *Critical Pedagogies and Theories for Post-Compulsory and Informal Education*. Liverpool: Public talk, Centre for Educational Research (CERES) Liverpool John Moores University, October 28, 2020.

Weber, M. (2004) *The Vocation Lectures*. Trans by Rodney Livingstone. Indianapolis and Cambridge: Hackett Publishing.

Wellmon, C. (2017) 'The University is Dead, Long Live the Academy! Reflections on the Future of Knowledge' *ABC Religion and Ethics*. www.abc.net.au/religion/the-university-is-dead-long-live-the-academy-reflections-on-the-/10095222. (Last accessed 20 January 2022).

Wilson, A. L. and Kiely, R. C. (2002) *Towards a Critical 7eory of Adult Learning/Education: Transformational Theory and Beyond*. Adult Education Research Conference. Paper 67. http://newprairiepress.org/aerc/2002/papers/67. (Last accessed 20 January 2022).

Part 5

Rhizome

Erudition in Times of Apnoea; Educating an Ill Generation

'It is difficult to tell a short-sighted man how to get somewhere'
(Wittgenstein, 1984:1e)

This is the concluding part of *Cultures of Erudition* and offers a critical reflection and further discussion of Synapses I, II, and III presented in previous parts. This part offers a space for debating a new index of adult education as erudition. It confirms the dynamic nature of the relational ties among individuals, institutions, and constructs (in education) that may be firm or fluid, fibrous and non-linear – rhizomatic, by means of returning to root and therefore radical. It moreover creates a hybrid topological geography of the learning network that accommodates erudition and ways this can be openly interpreted and practiced in adult education, with a particular focus on vocational and creative curricula. It draws from empirical studies in teaching an array of subjects at University level and eclectic readings that form relevant connections to the work of Deleuze and Guattari and contemporary pedagogy as well as eclectic synthesis of classical philosophy, literary work, and various curriculum theories. In previous parts the term scholar was presented as constitutive for the conception of a critical pedagogy towards erudition (by culture and by sensibility) (Pessoa, 2010:77) and as derivative of the Aristotelian term schole – the contemplative praxis of leisure that is not a passive state of idleness but a critical contribution to intellectual and political life, to citizenship and to pedagogy. The root for this critical contemplation of pedagogical present and futures is based on a symptomatological approach, and the malady of all maladies seems to be a sort of self-developed and self-sustained tiredness that is less of a load of the kind of productive labour or intellectual fatigue, which characterised modern times. On the contrary, the symptom that seems to be an uninspired and uninspiring tiredness is close to what Fernando Pessoa calls tedium in *The Book of Disquiet* (Pessoa, 2010). Pessoa's tedium however brings an

DOI: 10.4324/9781003220619-6

intensive and mysterious almost existentially and environmentally gener-
ated disquiet. The tedium which manifests in labour-less tiredness brings
a surprisingly rebellious response. It bring us to the observation of how
astonishingly inverted the phenomenon of tiredness can become when it
conditionally develops as a symptom of the pedagogical praxis and not as
an epiphenomenon of the practice of education in its formal setting.

Peter Handke in *The Jukebox & Other Essays on Storytelling* (1994)
makes a poetic yet critical association between tiredness and studentship,
appraising both in relation to each other, offering thus an intriguing cartography of their enigmatic (for the author) and anticipated (for the reader)
synthesis. In the rhetorical style dialogues that compile Hanke's 'Essay on
Tiredness' (Handke, 1994:3–46) the latter becomes a situated praxis. When
it becomes an event to take place in lecture halls, in the presence and idleness
of uninspiring 'banking' (Freire, 2017:48) infused by 'examination-oriented
pedantry, interspersed every now and then with a facetious undercurrent or
a malicious allusion addressed to those in the know' (Handke, 1994:5), it is
guilt-free and rebellious, and turned progressively through disquiet to exas-
peration. In the literary cosmos of Handke, the apprehended necessity of
enduring tedium as constitutive and compulsory praxis of becoming fit for
a future world one experiences, turns into indulge in aggression as means
for escaping. It encompasses a moment – in the least – of contemplative
praxis and reflection, an instant of breathing in and consequently a shock
in waking up from a state of pneumatic apnoea. The most important note
in Handke's text concerns the fact that tiredness and tedium have different
degrees less by means of intensity and more by means of quality and substance. Weariness, boredom, and fatigue, although symptomatically com-
parative, they are made of different substance and contribute to one's and
common life significantly. This is less a literary twist and more of a creative
interpretation of science. Peter Toohey in the book *Boredom: A Lively History* (2011) says there is a 'link between boredom and an agitated or angry
disposition' (Toohey, 2011:52) and that to be prone to boredom has 'perva-
sive effects on aggression' (Toohey, 2011:64), noting also that the malady
lies in chronic boredom associated more to neurosis and paranoia (Toohey,
2011:68) and less to sleepiness.

The scholar's tedium however is different. The exasperating tedium experienced in studentship is perhaps something a previous (but recent, post-war)
generation of Higher Education learners experienced. We often remember
this quite fondly and naively and perhaps realise we have romanticised it
as integral and distinctive part of a past scholarly life. It becomes progressively de-territorialised and obliviously stripped from any reference of institutional character, regardless of educational context, subject and country of
study or residence. For instance, 'while at University' is a very common

expression among then or current scholars who nod in agreement and with mindlessly mischievous and deeply empathetic understanding with no need or curiosity to identify a name of campus, year, or circumstantial data. It has become almost a commons by redolence and by a mystified acceptance that going to university means a necessary evil for cultivating adulthood. This acceptance involves an expectation that adult education may also 'evoke extreme disquiet' (Rabinbach, 1992:156) and one should expect to experience such even being sedentary, listening to a talk in Aula Magna, gazing at the water of Venice canals. As Handke – more or less controversially – implies in 'The Essay on Tiredness' (1994:3–46) the exasperated tedium and the disquiet of desire for erudition of the scholar has been part of the cultivating praxis to achieve humanity. The disquiet of desire used to postulate the importance of political emancipation through the jeopardy of responding to the maladies of an existing institutional system ontologically from within the remit of scholar and exercising the role and responsibility scholarship and studentship carry. This has changed progressively perhaps into what Mark Fisher names as the ontological quality of an ill generation that is being educated, will soon enrol, or has just graduated – 'reflexive impotence' (Fisher, 2009). This is a speculatively and empirically emerging comprehension of recent phenomena and the way they amplified the systemic maladies within and around adult education and pedagogy. This is seen as particularly related to professionally prescribed curricula. It may however also selectively and symptomatically apply to issues and pedagogical observations within non-formal, life-long learning and compulsory education and the wider context of ecological and political cultivation and culture as associated with the axiomatics of learning while living and experiencing by affect and by cognito (Pessoa's erudition by sensibility).

The jeopardy of critical scholarship – one's capacity to be reflective and contemplative while in studentship – is not attempted anymore or rather it is observed par exception and under very particular circumstances in which it often ends up becoming thoughtless activism. This seems to happen not because the phenomenon of expressing disquiet is evaluated as being unnecessary but because it is deemed as non-profitable. This is not a praxis (non-action) by economy or efficiency (by reference to the law of least effort) that would make it sustainable and ecological; this is an auto-immune condition of scholarly aboulia and desire-block. The symptom of aboulia was once attributed to a scholar's brain being intellectually suffering a burn-out, due to becoming subject to intellectual exhaustion by formal (and compulsory) education and was seen as developmental malady for modern society (Rabinbach, 1992:147). In fact, the relevant studies led to methodological distinction between a superior and an inferior learner (Rabinbach, 1992:152) and which of course would leave our maverick and temperate in the shadows.

Such symptomatic neurasthenia of intellectual slowness is now assigned to different immanently systemic maladies that are also triggering an epidemic of institutional changes with no transformative purpose or scope that can be foreseen as meaningful. Organisational initiatives to re-invent university pedagogy by the likes of umbrella block teaching or flipped classrooms, are often imposed by administrators and executive management as seen fit to cursorily align with institutional distinctiveness and to suit the educational demographic of incoming students. They end up in their majority as recurring and short-sighted trends in a circular and autotelic economy and mean no harm to studentship, as the learning relata rarely make anything of them. On the contrary, the scholars who implement those and are instructed to implement them in planned and lived curricula as well as any sliver of critical pedagogy left in between, end up also in tedium and idleness, feeling often bemused, stressed and rarely capable of carrying desire in inducing transformative praxis of any evocative kind.

The pedagogical question here is whether this tedium is potentially oppressive or progressive (or perhaps potentially both, ontologically complementing each other happening at different times) and how it can be channelled into becoming of the progressive kind in a thoughtful and inclusive – yet undeniably eclectic – manner. This is a critical and clinical question that involves not only the systematic observation of symptoms in the maladies of pedagogy (a nosology) but also a fearless and risky appreciation of the possibilities entailed in the creating a new future inherently by response to those symptoms, accepting that illness justifies life through the possibility for and appreciation of [better] health. To educate an ill generation and to create new pedagogies from and for it, means going beyond the rhetorical question posed by Mark Fisher, 'how has it become acceptable that so many people, and especially so many young people are ill?' (Fisher, 2009:19), which leads to the proposition that the malady lies in the fact that so stress as tedium are privatised and treated as 'incumbent on individuals to resolve' (Fisher, 2009:19). Concomitantly, the scholar is post-lexic, born into culture and bred into networks that are anti-mnemonic (Fisher, 2009:25). This 'post-lexia' (Fisher, 2009:25) is not only a symptom of pedagogical neurasthenia but also a sort of cultural allergy, an auto-immune disorder belonging ontologically to the age of the 'environmentally hypersensitive' (Colomina and Wigley, 2016:120–121). It is the same age when the mobile device becomes one's individual and collective sensorium and affective aid and as well as connecting and disconnecting it can also generate symptoms of anxiety related to a sense of self (Colomina and Wigley, 2016:243). This age of immunological hypersensitivity and 'no-mo-phobia' (Colomina and Wigley, 2016:243) is not open to the occurrence of otherness and hybridisation (Han, 2015:3) although we all are (trained to be) alert to notions of equality and diversity. The latter, which remain exceptionally important when understood by sensibility and openness, are bastardised by a progressively intensified hypersensitivity in matters of dignity and self-respect in controversial and under occasionally reversed terms. We observe then an affordance of victimisation and ill-willed entitlement of the scholar, who only lives in a fable of a people. The latter is a pseudo-network that is an alliance of fault-finding and expressing dissatisfaction in an a-politicised and short-sighted manner, not within the scope of hope for transformation, but because they have nothing to lose and to prove a point, which is a malady of its own merit.

Pedagogically, and symptomatologically, the self-indulgence of today's scholars-in-studentship (traditionally called learners or students) to engage in processes of victimisation while instead of becoming a people they form a clientele, takes place at the same time as another symptom – that of scholar paralysis. This apnoea of academic imagination belongs to Mark Fisher's ill generation of students with reflexive impotence (Fisher, 2009) and virally transmits into the rest of the relata in the praxis of pedagogy: the educators. The latter become blind by systemic changes that are on steroids, injustice concerning sector, class, and employment type, most notably precarious working. Otherwise driven by the desire to aspire, cultivate people-in-becoming, pedagogical sensitivities in the wider sense and rarely (why not) charisma in nurturing and instilling ethos and political responsibility, the collegia (scholars in the role of educators) are themselves exhausted and stressed, which is a pedagogical symptom widely observed and so often overlooked. To look optimistically to a pedagogically transformative future, we must position pedagogy within a sustainable educational ecosystem beyond its 'humanogenetic role' (Alexandre and Besnier, 2018:21) and not merely to assert a history of the humankind through tools and language and to perpetuate an achievement-obsessed society, because the 'imperative to achieve makes one sick' (Han, 2015:10) and to become sick means to assert the possibility of becoming healthy. A critical pedagogy of erudition and desire needs culture as restrictive and not as generative 'and prosthetic social apparatus' (Preciado, 2019:145). Only in such condition, education can acquire substance that is inter-relational and transhumanist (taking place among relata), and post-anthropocentric (taking place for people who allow for the immunological other). After all, even Aristotle's education as non-accumulative exaltation of the human intellect is both complicitly 'transindividual' (Raunig, 2010:116) and immanently situated – in the topos, the polis, and the ethos of the other, expanding polymorphous, rhizomatic and fabulative into the cosmos; it is a growing 'abstract machine of mutations' (Deleuze and Guattari, 1987:223).

References

Alexandre, L. and Besnier, J. M. (2018) *Do Robots Make Love? From AI to Immortality*. London: Octopus Books.

Colomina, B. and Wigley, M. (2016) *Are We Human: Notes on an Archaeology of Design*. Zurich: Lars Müller Publishers.

Deleuze, G. and Guattari, F. (1987) *A Thousand Plateaus: Capitalism and Schizophrenia*. Trans by B. Massumi. Minneapolis and London: University of Minnesota Press.

Fisher, M. (2009) *Capitalism Realism; Is There no Alternative?* Winchester: Zero Books.

Freire (2017) *Pedagogy of the Oppressed*. Trans by Myra Bergman Ramos. London: Penguin.

Han, B.-C. (2015) *The Burnout Society*. Stanford CA: The University of Stanford Press.

Handke, P. (1994) *The Jukebox and Other Essays on Story Telling*. Trans by Ralph Manheim and Krishna Winston. New York: Farrar, Straus, Giroux.

Pessoa, F. (2010) *The Book of Disquiet*. Trans by Margaret Jull Costa. London: Serpent's Tail.

Preciado, P. B. (2019) *An Apartment on Uranus*. London: Fitzcarraldo.

Rabinbach, A. (1992) *The Human Motor: Energy, Fatigue, and the Origins of Modernity*. Berkeley and Los Angeles: University of California Press.

Raunig, G. (2010) *A Thousand Machines*. Los Angeles: Semiotext(e).

Toohey, P. (2011) *Boredom: A Lively History*. New Haven and London: Yale University Press.

Wittgenstein, L. (1984) *Culture and Value*. Trans by P Winch. Chicago, IL: The University of Chicago Press.

Index

aboulia 2, 3, 13–15, 24, 48, 57
academy 11, 20, 33, 43, 44–46
activism 3, 9, 39, 57
Alexandre and Besnier 12, 20, 24, 59
Anthropocene 7, 14
Anti-Oedipus 14, 39
anxiety 23, 31, 58
Aoki, T. 8, 11, 13, 27, 36
arachnean 4, 15, 37, 38
Aristotle 4, 12, 19–21, 31, 33, 36, 59
assemblage 4, 8, 38, 43, 49
asthenia 15, 47
attention 22–23
autistic 23, 37, 47, 51
autotelic 10, 44, 58

banking 10, 22, 56
becoming 2, 5, 9, 10, 12, 15, 16, 20,
    22, 24, 31, 34, 35, 37–40, 44–46, 48,
    50–52, 56–59
bios politikos 20, 22, 25, 34
bios theoretikos *see* bios politikos
Book of Disquiet 2, 15, 21–22, 43, 55;
    see also disquiet
boredom 14, 22–24, 47, 56
Braidotti, R. 3, 5, 10, 35
Burnet, J. 19, 31, 33, 36
burnout 2, 14, 22–23

campus 1, 2, 57
capitalism 8, 13–14, 23, 36
capitalism realism 23, 36
cartographies 5, 14–15, 19, 27, 31, 43,
    48, 50, 56
choice theory 20

citizenship 5, 20, 25, 33–36, 38–40, 43,
    45, 47–49
civic disengagement 48–49
civic life 3, 34–35, 48; *see also* bios
    politikos
classroom 13, 45
clinical 15, 31, 48
Cole, D.R. 7, 10, 20, 26, 36, 44
collective responsibility 25
collegium 27, 33–34, 39, 44
commons 1–3, 14, 20, 32, 57
community xi, 26, 33–35, 37, 44
compassion 25, 26
consciousness 12, 44, 46
consumption 1, 25
contemplation 19, 20–22, 24–27, 31,
    33, 36, 38–40, 45–49, 55–57
contingency 9, 47, 49
counter-cartography 4, 27
COVID-19 *see* pandemic
critical pedagogy 3, 15, 22, 34, 36,
    38–39, 48–50, 55, 58–59
cultivation 3, 12, 19, 22, 33, 39, 57
culture 3, 8, 11, 13, 22–23, 25–27,
    31–35, 39, 40, 43–50, 55, 57–59
currere 8, 11, 15, 19, 26–27, 31–34,
    39–40, 43–49, 51
curriculum 3, 7–8, 11, 13, 19, 26–27,
    31, 34, 36, 44–45, 47, 49, 51, 55
cyborg 14, 34, 45, 49

de Botton, A. 8, 43
Deleuze and Guattari 4, 14, 27, 37–38,
    55, 59
Deligny, F. 5, 31, 37–38, 51

democracy 3, 25, 33–36, 43, 45, 47
desire 3–5, 15, 19–21, 24–25, 27, 31,
    34–40, 43, 45, 47, 50, 51, 57–59
Dewey, J. 21, 34–35
disclosive 27, 46–47
discourse ethics 34
disquiet 1–3, 15, 21–23, 34–35, 43,
    55–57
diversity 11, 35, 38, 59

eclectic 2, 55, 58
ecology 4–5, 7, 8, 11, 13, 15, 19, 21,
    25, 27, 33, 38, 44, 47
economy 15, 25–26, 34, 47, 57, 58
ecstasy 25; *see also* immersion
emancipation 3, 22, 26, 34–35, 46, 57
entourage 50–51
environment 22, 24–27, 32, 45, 49–50
environmental sciences 32
erudition 3–5, 11–16, 19, 21–27, 31–34,
    36–39, 43–48, 50–51, 55, 57, 59
ethics 12, 19, 33–34, 36, 43–44, 47
event 8, 14, 19, 27, 31, 35, 38–39, 46, 56
evolution 10–11, 44, 46
exhaustion 13, 23–24, 36, 57
experience 2, 8, 11, 13, 22–23, 26–27,
    32, 34, 39, 48, 52
experiential poverty 15

fabulative 59
fatigue 15, 55–56
Fisher, M. 4, 13, 15, 23–24, 33, 36, 47,
    57–59
forces of control 50
freedom 1–2, 21, 49
Freire, P. 9–11, 22, 24, 39, 52, 56
Frichot, H. 4, 8

Giroux, H.A. 3, 19, 26, 33, 36, 39

Habermas, J. 34
Han, B.-C. 4, 14–15, 20–26, 47, 59
Higher Education 20, 23, 32, 56
history 3, 12, 56
hope 20, 26, 39, 46
Human Motor 15, 23

identity 3, 38, 44
idiocracy 11–12
idleness 3, 21, 36, 55–56, 58

ignorance 46–49
illness 3, 13–14, 21, 23, 25, 36, 48–49, 58
imagination 21, 39, 49, 59
immanence 8, 10, 44, 50–51, 58–59
immersion 22, 24–25, 31; *see also*
    ecstasy
immunological 7, 14, 58–59
institution 7, 8, 21, 37, 39, 43–44,
    56–58
intelligence 10–12, 19, 46

knowledge xi, xii, 3, 10, 20, 22–23, 36,
    39, 43–44, 46

labour 15, 25, 45, 47, 50, 55–56
learner 3, 5, 10–15, 23–24, 27, 31, 34,
    36–37, 39, 43, 56, 59
leisure 1, 20–21, 24, 49, 55
lifelong learning 1, 10, 23, 34–35, 50

machine 13, 15, 23, 32, 48, 49
malady 3, 15, 23, 26, 37, 45, 55–59
maverick 5, 15, 43, 48–52, 57
modernity 15, 23, 25
multiplicities 27, 38, 51

nature-culture continuum 32, 34, 40
network 5, 15, 31, 37–39, 43, 49–51,
    55, 59
neurasthenia 15, 23, 25, 36, 58
neurological crisis 14, 23
neurosis *see* paranoia
Nichomachean Ethics 12
nomad 3, 5, 24, 43, 51

oikos 7, 8
onto-ecology 4, 27
oppression 9, 43

pandemic 7, 14
paranoia 56
pathologies 3, 4, 14, 31
pediagogy 40, 52
people-in-becoming 5, 9, 15, 31, 37,
    43, 50–51
periphery 49–50
Pessoa, F. 2–4, 15, 19, 21–22, 34, 43, 55
Plato 12, 33
policy 11, 22
post-anthropocentric 34

post-human 5, 10, 14, 31–33, 35, 37–39, 45–46
practicum 14, 47–50; *see also* labour
Preciado, P. B. 20, 24, 43
procrastination 25
Protagoras 12
PSRB 34, 51

Rabinbach, A. 2–3, 15, 23–25, 36, 47, 57
radical 4, 8–9, 15, 38, 44–45, 47, 48, 55
Ranciere, J. 46–47
reality 2–3, 9, 15, 21, 26–28, 37–38
reflexive impotence 13–14, 24, 33, 47–49, 57–59
relata 3, 5, 38, 40, 43–47, 49–52, 58–59
relationality 35, 37, 39, 44
resistance 3, 38
risk 8–9, 33, 38
root 8–9, 46, 55
Roy, K. 3–4, 51

SBS *see* shifting baseline syndrome
scholar 5, 23, 45–46, 48–50, 55, 57–59
schole 3, 20–24, 26, 31, 34–35, 45–46, 49–50, 55
Semetsky, I. 4, 20, 26–27
sensibility 22–23, 26, 34, 36–37, 39, 43–44, 46, 51, 55, 57, 59
shifting baseline syndrome 32
silence 9, 50
situatedness 3, 13, 26–27, 35–38, 40, 46, 52, 56, 59

stress 13–14, 23–24, 33–34, 38, 44, 58
studentship 2, 3, 33, 55–59
sustainability xi, 7
symptom 4, 48, 55–59
synthesis 4, 8–9, 19, 24, 55–56
system 2, 5, 11, 13, 27, 32, 39, 44, 48, 51, 57–59

tedium 2–3, 14, 15, 21–24, 45, 47, 55–58
temperate 5, 15, 43, 48–52, 57
thanato-technics 47
theoria 12, 15, 31
thinkables 8, 36
Thousand Plateaus, A 15
tool-enhancement 13, 15
topology 7, 35, 49, 52, 55
Tynan, A. 4, 48–49

utopian pedagogy 31, 38–40, 45–47

virtual 27, 39
virtue 20, 33
vocation 4, 10, 12, 14, 20, 24, 32, 34, 44–45, 48–52, 55

Wallin, J. 4, 7, 8, 27, 44
Webb, D. 4, 39–40, 45–46
Whitehead 22, 27

Zeitgeist 9–10
Zembylas, M. 4, 27, 38, 39

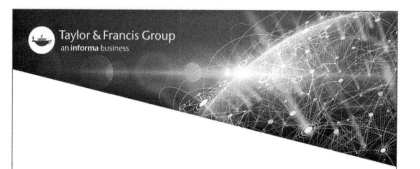

www.ingramcontent.com/pod-product-compliance
Ingram Content Group UK Ltd.
Pitfield, Milton Keynes, MK11 3LW, UK
UKHW020427010325
455677UK00029B/1029